JOURNALING
as a Spiritual Practice

Tracing the Lines of Grace to God's Presence

Allison Byxbe

Moody Publishers
Chicago

All emphasis in Scripture has been added.

Published in association with Don Pape for Pape Commons.

Edited by Ashleigh Slater
Interior design: Faceout Studio, Paul Nielsen
Cover design: Kaylee Lockenour Dunn

Author photo: Jonathan Hawley

ISBN: 978-0-8024-4100-3

Originally delivered by fleets of horse-drawn wagons, the affordable paperbacks from D. L. Moody's publishing house resourced the church and served everyday people. Now, after more than 125 years of publishing and ministry, Moody Publishers' mission remains the same—even if our delivery systems have changed a bit. For more information on other books (and resources) created from a biblical perspective, go to www.moodypublishers.com or write to:

Moody Publishers
820 N. LaSalle Boulevard
Chicago, IL 60610

1 3 5 7 9 10 8 6 4 2

Printed in the United States of America

For Ben, Reed, Lucas, and Ansley
You are the best lines of grace running
through my story.

Contents

Introduction

The Spiritual Practice
That Became My Lifeline to God

Fill your paper with the breathings of your heart.

~William Wordsworth

"Have you tried writing it down?" I asked my friend. She laughed a little, shaking her head. I'm sure she expected that question from me. She knows I love to journal. I have almost my whole life. And it seems journaling is growing in popularity, which makes me, a pen-to-page loving woman, happy.

Experts have been showing us for decades the tried-and-true benefits of putting pen to page. Journaling lowers stress; improves our physical, mental, emotional, and spiritual health; and can be an effective tool for reducing anxiety and depression. The embodied practice of writing down our thoughts, processing our experiences, and using our creativity to imagine possibilities is the type of practice that can form us in spiritually significant ways.

For some of us, though, journaling can be an elusive, on-again-off-again habit that seems to slip through the cracks too easily. Journaling becomes another task on the to-do list instead of the life-giving, soul-expanding gift it can be.

I'm hoping you picked up this book because, like me, you're a pen-to-page loving person too—or you want to be. If so, I should let you know this isn't your typical journaling book. It's not just journaling how-to, though you will find that in here. It's also a creative and imaginative exploration and analysis of metaphors. Why metaphors? Because Scripture's metaphors were my pathway back to a renewed faith and love for God.

The Bible, with its richly layered language, is steeped in metaphors. From the earliest writings in Genesis describing God as breath, to Elijah's experience with God in the gentle whisper, to Jesus referring to Himself as living water and the bread of life, and to the experience of the Holy Spirit as a dove and as fire, Scripture leans on metaphor to illuminate the presence of God. Imagine the spiritual wholeness we can embody when journaling through Scripture's metaphors illuminates the presence of God.

In this book, you'll come to see how you're probably already more familiar with metaphors than you think—and that they're more important to how you feel and navigate life than you might realize. You'll discover how to spot metaphors in Scripture, and not just that journaling matters, but *why*. You'll explore the spiritual growth possible when you bring journaling and Scripture's metaphors together. And, you'll learn the practical how-to of establishing and maintaining this journaling practice that deepens and sustains your relationship with God.

This book is an invitation into the richness of God's imagination, creativity, and words to discover His presence with us, right here, right now, in the stories we're living.

In these pages, I also invite you into the story that changed everything in my life. As I write these words, fourteen years have passed since our family's uncertainties about our son Reed's struggles and delays were diagnosed with a string of letters and numbers that began to rewrite our reality. I've written about that time, his diagnosis, and the grief we've lived through hundreds of times in my private journal and publicly in online spaces. I've led journaling workshops sharing his story, our journey, and how journaling through it all brought me back to God. So why keep writing about it now in this book you're holding? Because it's still rewriting me, and I pray it will lend you some hope too.

This book is an invitation into the richness of God's imagination, creativity, and words to discover His presence with us, right here, right now, in the stories we're living.

I continue to search for words to wrap around the grief and love, the joy and sorrow, the sobs and splitting laughter, the wounding and the healing, the rock-bottom places and the bottomless grace, the dying and the resurrection. *The broken, blessed, and given*, as Eugene Peterson has said.[1]

In my journal, I write down the solitary word *broken*, and tears slide down my cheek. This word names how I have felt. Inching over just a bit on the page, I write *blessed*. My heart hitches and questions circle around it like a hungry vulture. I ask in my journal, "Is a broken life a blessed one?" My pen hovers over this pressing paradox. Then, I scrawl out *given* just beyond the first two words. I recognize that even in what we've lost, we have been given so much, because God's grace is so intricately woven into each line. And now, out of my broken and blessed life, I give—we hold out for others—the hope I have in Christ.

With as much fallible certainty as one human can have, I know our family's story is the beautiful ache through which I've been reborn. It's a strange thing to hold in one hand the utter conviction that I would in one skinny, hot second trade anything for my son to live free of all the brokenness that his diagnosis bears. And on the other hand? To hold the deepest gratitude that he is a straight-up miracle. To try to pull the two apart would leave us with no story at all. I could never have known myself, my marriage, my children, or my God in all their beauty apart from walking this path.

There's healing possible when we put pen to page and imagine all that God is able to do in us and through us.

Perhaps there are lines written into your life that are confusing or upending. Maybe you're looking for a way to make sense of the part of your story you find yourself in. I'd love to take your hand and help you see through journaling the compassionate hand of God that is writing goodness and beauty into your story.

In the beginning, God spoke creation into existence with His breath, with His words. And God's first gift to human beings, to all of us who are born, is breath. In the beginning, God made dirt breathe. And as fragile as things made of dirt might be, we have the resilient, eternal, life-giving breath of God within us. Each one of us—regardless of what we've experienced, what we believe, or how close to rock bottom we've gotten—has His breath in us. That small, rhythmic, quiet reminder that God is with us. This book, then, is your invitation to imagine that life can be breathed and written into dead places. To believe that your breath and your words hold more hope than you might dare imagine.

If you need a gentle, honest, seasoned friend to walk alongside you as you learn to breathe words onto the pages of your journal, then you're in the right place. I don't have all the answers and can't fix everything that may have gone off course for you. But I can show you a way forward to process the hard things that have disconnected you from God. I can help you learn how to immerse yourself in the metaphors of life and Scripture to experience the real, living, breathing presence of Emmanuel. I can walk with you and show you the healing that's possible when through our writing we imagine all that God is able to do in us and through us.

And if your story isn't one you are trying to make sense of right now, but instead, you love journaling or are simply intrigued to see how you can make it a spiritual practice that will bring you closer to God, keep reading. I'm so excited to come alongside you and share this gift with you!

So, what about you? Have *you* tried writing it down? If you're ready for a fresh way to experience the presence of God, then take a deep breath with me, turn the page, and begin a journey that I think could just change everything.

CHAPTER 1

The Potential of Metaphor:

You Can't Pour New Wine into Old Wineskins

I do not believe that sheer suffering teaches. If suffering alone taught, all the world would be wise, since everyone suffers. To suffering must be added mourning, understanding, patience, love, openness, and the willingness to remain vulnerable. All these and other factors combined, if the circumstances are right, can teach and can lead to rebirth.

~Anne Morrow Lindbergh

I sat at my kitchen table, on an ordinary day in August 2011, scrolling through Pinterest. When my husband, Ben, answered his phone, I froze. We'd been waiting on this call about Reed from the pediatrician for over a month. Though Ben was only nodding and scribbling notes, I could tell the results showed something.

Hanging up the phone, he turned to tell me the news: a rare genetic disorder. Three extra chromosomes. A spectrum of possibilities but physical and intellectual difficulties guaranteed. Apraxia. Hypotonia. Possible heart issues. Anxiety. Recurring pneumonia. Of course, our pediatrician advised us not to Google the syndrome, and of course, I didn't listen.

I was a first-time mom to the cutest, curly, red-headed little boy, and suddenly now, trying to grasp the story of a genetic disorder that would rewrite every aspect of our family's life. On the genetic report 49xxxxy was the name of his disorder, if you could even call that a name. Really, it was just a string of numbers and letters only recognizable to genetics experts. Most doctors, we were warned, would not have much, if any, real experience with this diagnosis.

With no language to explain what we were dealing with or even experts to turn to, my fear and grief began to rise. Desperate to make sense of this unknown, strange reality I found myself in, I scoured Google for the answers I hoped would help me find my footing. But Google only answered back with stark medical reports and terrifying statistics, instead of the reassurance that I so desperately hoped for.

Beneath the fear was a profound anger toward God. And my journal was peppered with questions. Why did He allow this to happen to our son? In an already difficult world, why add so much more to a tiny boy's plate? Why us? Why him? Why did so many other people not have to walk this path?

Even though God had blessed me with a husband I loved, work I was passionate about, and a home I enjoyed, this shattering news stood out as a glaring breach of trust. *I had played by the rules and now God was breaking them.*

I found myself thinking things I wasn't ready to say out loud, and so I wrote them down in my journal: The God I thought I knew, understood, and trusted had become strange, contradictory, and untrustworthy. I turned inward, to myself, to make sense of the unfathomable. Questions haunted me on every side.

When life went unbearably sideways, I found myself living in a story that I never would have written, enduring hard lines that I'd rather write out of the story.

A normal, healthy, typically developing son? No.

My son being playmate to my friends' babies? Impossible.

More babies for us? How could I dare risk this happening again?

Enjoying the empty nest, golden years with my husband? No guarantee.[1]

When life went unbearably sideways with this rare diagnosis, I found myself living in a story that I never would have written, enduring hard lines that I'd rather write out of the story. One minute I happily held the dreams of a normal, healthy, typical childhood for our son. In the next, those dreams dissolved into the harsh reality of missed milestones, therapies, hospitalizations, and miles of questions with no answers.

And my relationship with God flatlined.

It's perhaps unfair to blame the whole of my disconnect from God only on this diagnosis. My faith had been limping along for four years. In 2007, my older sister

Erin learned at thirty-six weeks' gestation that her baby—my niece Zoey—had died. I was devastated. After unexplained infertility and unsuccessful fertility treatments and then many months of prayers, Erin surprisingly became pregnant with Zoey without any outside intervention. We were ecstatic. God had heard our prayers, we reasoned, so why eight short months later were those answered prayers being taken back? What kind of cruel joke could this be?

My vibrant faith in a good, loving, life-giving God was shaken to its core. As I watched Erin shoulder this impossible grief, my spirit sagged under its weight too. For the first time in my very manageable, neat, tidy life of faith, I could not find a way forward in the face of an unfairness that shattered my illusion of control. *Did I really believe all those things I had professed so easily about God? Was any of it ever really true?* I had operated under the assumption that if I prayed hard enough, faithfully enough, righteously enough, my prayers could keep this sort of thing far from me and my family.

In the microcosm of hearing that my niece was stillborn, nothing else was still. Not the frantic phone calls. Not the dropping of everything else to go be in the hospital. Not the rushed planning and painful questions. Not the labor that still had to be done for Erin to deliver her baby. Not the tears coursing down cheeks and sobs heaving through bodies. None of it was still.

But stillborn was an apt word to describe my brake-slammed, whip-lashed faith. I sat so still, straining to hear my own heart beating. Would we live again after this unspeakable loss? It was hard to fathom.

At my kitchen table in 2011, with Zoey's death still threaded through my heart, the crisis of Reed's diagnosis crushed my faith. How had I so naively believed that one traumatic loss in our family would save us from another? Ben and I sat side-by-side, shell-shocked, in the low light of our basement, for hours after the pediatrician's phone call. We didn't speak; we silently grieved what would never be, with the curly-topped baby who slept in the next room completely unaware of how our gravity had shifted.

A lie had been planted in my heart: God could not be trusted for good things. And if He was near, He could not be trusted to help.

On that August day in 2011, all I wanted was to go back to the life I had before the diagnosis came crashing into our lives. Instead, I was forced to stay right where I was in the raw, gritty newness of my son's overwhelming diagnosis.

I couldn't reconcile the life I used to have with the reality of special needs that would influence every detail of our current lives and whatever future was left for us. I was in a place I didn't know with no clear map to navigate my way through. I couldn't weave together the fragments of my reality fast enough to stay above water. In my numb disbelief, my emotional and spiritual well-being plummeted me into a spiritual no-man's land.

In the midst of my spiritual crisis, I longed for the comfort of my faith to return, as I grieved and tried to piece my heart back together. But as anyone who has faced significant loss can attest, you simply can't go back. You can't unknow what you've learned, which is its own kind of grief. It is as if you're knocking furiously on the door of a house from which you've been evicted. You can still see the warmth of light flooding out of the windows; you can see all the other house guests warmly ensconced in their safe, cozy environment, but you're out in the cold.

You may also know loss, disappointment, setback, or grief. While the details of your story may be different from mine, my guess is you long to reconnect with God too—and I want to help you. What if I showed you how journaling through Scripture's metaphors to experience God's presence is one way to do that? If you're ready to revive your faith through this journaling practice I've developed, the place to start is by understanding what metaphors are and how they work.

What Exactly Is Metaphor?

If high school English class was the last time you thought much about metaphor, then lean in. Instead of dissecting metaphors in literature, I want to show you how to see the transformative nature of metaphor in your very own life. I'll define metaphor and show you the places where this figurative language is already showing up in your life. You'll discover how we need metaphors to make sense of the world we're in, the lives we lead, and the faith we have.

We need metaphors to make sense of the world we're in, the lives we lead, and the faith we have.

Take for instance nicknames. Did you have one growing up? I had several, like Allie, Allie Cat, and Alice in Wonderland. One in particular stands out.

My dad loves to tell this story from my elementary school days. As responsible parents do, mine set an 8 p.m. bedtime for me during the school year. My dad, as most reasonable parents might do, often stayed up until 10 or 11 p.m. As he would pass my bedroom late in the evening on his way to bed, I would call out, "Dad! I'm sound awake!"

Dad consistently responded, "Close your eyes little night owl, ask God to help you sleep. Goodnight, I love you." Of course, my dad did not mean I was literally a creature with big round eyes and soft feathers sitting awake on the branches of a tree at night. But the endearing nickname created a story around my late-night tendencies that still gets shared around the Christmas dinner table.

The *Oxford English Dictionary* says that a metaphor, as figurative language, is "a word or phrase [that] is transferred to an object or action different from, but analogous to, that to which it is literally applicable."[2] In other words, we take a familiar idea and apply it to an idea or person or event that we're trying to understand.

Have you ever tried to explain a thunderstorm to a frightened child? "That's just the sky bowling," I remember hearing as a child. Has a friend ever tried to explain her grief to you? "My grief came wave after wave, but I never knew how big the wave would be or how long it would last." These are metaphors, and they are how we name and rename our experiences for ourselves and for others to create understanding. As writer Orson Scott Card is credited with saying, "Metaphors have a way of holding the most truth in the least space."[3]

Aristotle defines metaphor even more simply as "the process of 'giving the thing a name that belongs to something else.'"[4] We do this so intuitively, we may not even question or think twice about the metaphors we use. I sure didn't in my early years of teaching college writing classes.

"There's more than one way to skin a cat, y'know?" I said, eying a young woman in the back row of my professional communication class, her eyes bulging over my comment. She covered her mouth as a horrified gasp escaped. Either she thought I had literal experience skinning cats, or she found my figurative language offensive. Apparently, my humor was misplaced that day.

I'd grown up hearing that phrase my whole life, so the metaphor was normal to me. No one in my family had ever skinned a cat (to my knowledge) but somehow, somewhere I'd picked up the idea that if there was more than one way to do something, then the cat phrase applied.

Metaphorically speaking, all I meant that day in class was my students could accomplish their writing assignment in more than one way. In an instant, the power of metaphors crystallized for me. When they don't work, conversations go sideways, and people think you're weird or perhaps need therapy. When they do work, they deliver new perspectives and understanding quickly and memorably.

The skinned cat metaphor may have failed me in class that day, but I'm convinced that metaphors have the potential to change our lives. I know what you're probably thinking, *She teaches writing, for heaven's sake. Of course she'd say that.* I won't deny it—a love for words and language and their power to change our lives is at the core of what I believe. But I've also lived it. Metaphor has changed my life, and I fully believe it has the potential to reorient your heart, mind, and soul too.

The good news is metaphor isn't some new language you have to learn. Metaphors are baked into our everyday language. James Geary has reported that we use at least six metaphors *a minute*![5] Did you realize our normal, everyday conversations were so steeped in figurative language? Have you noticed the metaphors already woven into this chapter?

Once you start looking, you'll notice metaphor everywhere. Lakoff and Johnson show us how metaphor is baked into relationship language: "Their relationship is *in really good shape*. Their marriage is *on its last leg*."[6] Relationships, of course, don't have a physical body or shape, so how can they be in good shape, right? Relationships don't actually have legs, but we often borrow tangible language to describe something more abstract. This borrowing is how we make sense of something that may otherwise be difficult to describe or understand.

Journaling helps us connect to the God who calls Himself the Word.

Journaling as a spiritual practice to reconnect with God starts with appreciating the potential for metaphor to build and grow our imagination for what is possible, hopeful, and true. Even though we use metaphors regularly, we often do so subconsciously. We're not fully aware of using them, their impact on our thinking, or even why they communicate so effectively (or in my case in that classroom, ineffectively). But let me be clear. This isn't a grammar or literature book. This is a book that will show you the prevalence of metaphors, why they're so powerful, and how journaling through them might just change our lives. Writing is a practice that cultivates hope and healing within us. Journaling helps us connect to the God who calls Himself the Word.

How Metaphor Works

The *Merriam-Webster Dictionary* explains that metaphor comes from the Greek word *metapherein* ("to transfer").[7] When we speak or write in metaphor, we transfer our understanding of something known to something unknown. This transfer is essential to ground us in our current realities.

Think of a newborn, just moments before birth, encased in the warm, rhythmic cocoon of her mother's womb, then thrust into a waterless, gravity-laden space. Instinctively, the newborn cries to be heard, and her arms reach out, searching for the edges of her new reality. The baby is then swaddled by nurses in a soft blanket, mimicking as best as can be, the small, safe space of the mother's womb, because we know that babies need comfort.

Transformed from one reality to another, the newborn's understanding of warmth, comfort, and safety has been expanded. If the newborn could form articulate thoughts, she might say, "I like being wrapped up like this. I'm warm and my arms are pressed against my body, and someone is now gently, rhythmically shooshing me. This is a lot like where I've come from, but also different." Instead of an articulated thought, this new knowledge is expressed as the baby's cries quiet, and her body relaxes into her mother's arms. The baby is calmed and soothed because the transfer of knowledge in this new experience has succeeded.

As any new parent can attest, the baby will need to relearn and re-experience this knowledge hundreds or thousands of times as her body and experiences grow. This one moment of soothing will soon be interrupted by more crying, more learning, and more stretching to figure out how to exist in a new moment.

This is how we all grow. First, we experience something new. Then, we process the experience. We assimilate and translate the experiences, linking one to the next, creating a new understanding that is both a mixture of what we already know and what we are beginning to learn. This is the work of metaphor, to be the translator and medium that holds space between what has been and what is becoming.

Metaphors That Tell Stories

Metaphor is the bread and butter of life. We come into this world seeking to know and be known, to hear and be heard, to feel and be felt, and metaphors are one of the primary ways we create stories and templates to be known and to know.

Each metaphor can contain a universe of stories and become the building blocks for the stories through which we frame our lives. As Aundi Kolber describes, "The stories we weave and the meaning we make from them create templates for how we understand God, life, others, and ourselves."[8]

Parables can meet us right where we are and refract light from just the right angle to illuminate the darkness.

Sometimes, our stories feel too ordinary or mundane and we long for something more. Or, we find ourselves in a new season, unsure how to move forward. And then, other times, the stories we've been living start splintering and cracking or maybe even imploding right before our eyes, leaving us reeling and disoriented. We find ourselves living in stories that we never would have written, and somehow trying to make our way through.

An ancient parable became the first tiny thread of hope I'd find in the wake of Reed's diagnosis. Parables are stories of very ordinary things, and this is in part why they are so compelling, and are, as James Geary defines them, "narrated metaphor."[9] Eugene Peterson writes, "A parable is not ordinarily used to tell us something new but to get us to notice something we have overlooked."[10] Parables can meet us right where we are and refract light from just the right angle to illuminate the darkness.

A brief theological note before we move forward. In the following section, I am not asking you to reinterpret Jesus' original meaning for this parable. I am not trying to commit heresy! Instead, I'm inviting you to see the richness of the metaphor in the parable.

You Can't Pour New Wine into Old Wineskins

In the gospel of Luke, Jesus tells the Pharisees this parable:

> "No one tears a piece out of a new garment to patch an old one. Otherwise, they will have torn the new garment, and the patch from the new will not match the old. And no one pours new wine into old wineskins. Otherwise, the new wine will burst the skins; the wine will run out and the wineskins will be ruined. No, new wine must be poured into new wineskins. And no one after drinking old wine wants the new, for they say, 'The old is better.'" (Luke 5:36–39)

Jesus is making a theological contrast between their old religious way and His new life-giving way. He's inviting them into a new story, one that will stretch them beyond the story they've always known. But the reward? Knowing God in a deeply more personal way than they had ever known Him before. Similarly, I felt like God was inviting me into a new story with Reed's diagnosis, a story so different than the one I'd known or imagined I'd have. This ancient parable helped illuminate the reality I found myself in and gave me words to begin understanding what was happening to me.

I was trying desperately to get back home to myself, to who I thought I'd be as a parent, to what my marriage was like in all its youthful optimism before this diagnosis became an unwanted guest in our lives. I wanted to patch the old me up, but there didn't seem much of her left to put back together. All I had were just shreds of a person and a life that used to be.

I wanted to pour my new story into the old wineskin of my life, but I knew in my heart it wouldn't work. Every time I tried, the old container just couldn't hold it. What I needed but couldn't yet reconcile was who I had become in light of the loss that had marked me. If I kept trying to clamor back to who I was before this diagnosis, to inhabit my old skin, I would burst at the seams. That old skin was not built for this new reality. Instead, I needed to find a way to bridge between the person I had been and the person I was becoming, to let God dwell with me there in my new skin. To have, as Eugene Peterson says, "a realization of grace . . . [that] God was in this place"[11] even if I couldn't see it yet.

My training as an English professor helped me understand a metaphor's potential to deliver truth in a startling, profound way, bridging the gap between what we know and what we do not yet understand; of making the intangible knowable, of giving us new skin to pour new life into. But the question loomed large in front me, the same question that is asked of all who find themselves far from God: *Can we find God's presence again in bewildering places?*

In the beginning, I believed that three-minute phone call from our pediatrician had shattered all good possibilities for my life. And while it would take years of fumbling through the darkness and wrestling with difficult questions, God in His gracious, compassionate mercy would show me that phone call was just the opening to a richer, more complex, and ultimately more beautiful story. And, in the process, He would use metaphors to help me write new stories in my places of loss and suffering so that I could reconnect my heart and life back to Him.

JOURNALING PROMPTS

Instructions

When we live much of our lives on the surface (e.g., What am I going to have for lunch today? How does this shirt look on me? Did I remember to sign the form that's due today?), we may miss out on deeper thinking and awareness that is vital for healing and growth. Journaling helps us see the deeper aspects of mind and heart and cultivate an awareness that God is here.

The first two prompts can be done with just a few moments of your time. Consider doing them all in one day or completing one a day over the course of a week. The third prompt may take a bit more time, but you can always decide ahead of time how much time you want to journal for, set a timer for that amount, and then simply stop when the timer is done. For those new to journaling, timing your journal writing can be especially beneficial in reducing overwhelm.

Prompt 1

Consider spending one day intentionally jotting down the metaphors you encounter. You could even begin with some of the ones you may have noticed in this chapter. What happened as you began paying attention to the metaphors around you?

Prompt 2

Fill in each of the following blanks:

1. A word that describes my connection to God is . . .

2. If I named my current inner landscape as a color, it would be . . .

3. The unwanted guest in my life is . . .

4. When I think of the wineskin parable, what comes to mind is . . .

Prompt 3

Close your eyes. Breathe deeply. Allow yourself a few moments of quiet and stillness, where all you hear, all you feel, is your steady inhale and exhale. Ask God to open your imagination to Him.

Bring to mind a moment from your life that you'd consider a new wine–old wineskin experience. Perhaps a moment where you knew life would never be the same. A moment where you began to grapple with who you were becoming in light of the loss or difficulty or experience that marked you. How did you experience that moment?

Then, imagine God stitching together for you a new wineskin that is strong and sturdy. That can fully and safely hold you, your experience, your pain, and all you are becoming. And while this new skin is strong and sturdy, it is also soft and easy to hold, with His presence woven into every fiber.

Allow yourself to stay in the stillness and quiet of this intimacy with God. Then, when you're ready, can you journal about this experience?

Note.

If any of this feels overwhelming, give yourself permission to stop at any point.

CHAPTER 2

The Presence of God Through Metaphor:

The Unexpected, Gentle Whisper

God is always whispering—always.
It is my highest calling to draw near and listen.

~J. D. Walt

Just three weeks before Reed's diagnosis, our small family moved from South Carolina to Pennsylvania, away from our families and friends to a new town, with new jobs, a new church, and now a new diagnosis.

Weeks after we made this move, an earthquake, Hurricane Sandy, and an unusually heavy October snowstorm swept through our new town. I felt like Elijah standing on the mountainside wondering what on earth God was doing.

Is it possible to find God's presence in bewildering places of lost dreams and upending realities?

My son was not supposed to be disabled. I was not supposed to be a parent to a child with special needs. Motherhood was supposed to be an entirely different experience than the one I was having. I wanted the experience I saw so many of our friends having with their healthy, typical babies.

As the months after diagnosis ticked by, life felt more complicated, and less and less like the life I wanted to live. It spiraled with greater intensity, and I hunkered down and plowed through months of medical, specialist, and therapeutic appointments with our son.

When Hard Gets Harder

At just over a year old, Reed was hospitalized with pneumonia. We didn't know then that these hospitalizations would become a routine part of his childhood. Over the past decade, I've lost count of exactly how many times we've walked through hospital doors because pneumonia has held a vice grip on his lungs or because he needed surgery to correct yet another way his body was not functioning properly. But by my best estimations, Reed has been hospitalized somewhere between fifteen to twenty times.

Amid the steep learning curve of being a special needs mom, a small surprise came our way. One cold December night, I shakily removed the packaging around a pregnancy test. I followed the instructions, waited the prescribed minutes, and then saw a second pink line appear. The smallest bud of hope tried to peek through my tender, raw heart, but worry and fear could not be crowded out. What if this child also had a diagnosis?

We cautiously began sharing news of another baby with family after we heard the heartbeat at our six-week appointment. We started wondering whether we'd have a boy or a girl this time and holding tentative hope in our hearts for this new life.

I vacillated, sometimes by the minute, between hope and terror. The geneticist said our chances of another one of our children having a diagnosis like Reed's was extremely rare. But when you already had one child with a *rare* diagnosis (1 in 100,000 births), the doctor's assurances seemed thin and cold.

We would never find out if the geneticist was right about that baby. At the ten-week appointment, the ultrasound was silent and still. I couldn't trust God for good endings, and now, I couldn't trust my body to do the one thing that's uniquely a woman's to do.

Moving to a new state, receiving Reed's diagnosis, and experiencing a miscarriage all back to back left me reeling. I knew how impossibly far from God I felt, and each loss and setback made it seem less and less likely that I'd find Him in the pain and confusion of our reality.

Metaphors as Maps

While pain and confusion may make us lose our way from God's presence, metaphor can be a bridge back to finding Him. Commenting on Lauren Winner's book *Wearing God*, Jonathan Peterson surmises that metaphor "changes and deepens [us] if we pray to a God who is as close to us as clothing . . . a God who arrests our attention like flame."[1] The tangible nature of wearing clothes and experiencing the light of a fire can become real sign posts pointing us on our way to finding God once again.

Just the mention of flame, and my mind goes to the fire pit my husband, Ben, built in our backyard. As one of my favorite places to relax and be together as a family in the late fall season, my gaze is always drawn to its flickering flames, soothed by its warm dance. What about you? Where is your mind drawn when you think about warm, dancing flames?

With just a small bit of imagination, our minds can map almost any visceral experience to our less tangible experiences of God. Maybe our souls soften to His presence, familiar to us as our favorite fall sweater. Perhaps our hearts fill as we recognize God's sense of delight in the lilt of our children's laughter. Maybe, as our gaze is drawn to the fire, we are drawn in by the glimpses we catch of God's presence in the tangible. These places, these experiences, these everyday items become the directional markers, our True North, pointing us to God again and again, if we simply pay attention. What if we see that our daily experiences are the symbols in the map's legend showing us our way back to God?

Metaphors fill our everyday realities and are also woven throughout Scripture. In the Bible, we see God's presence in a burning bush, in a gentle whisper, as living water, and as the bread of life. Ott explains that metaphors act as "communicative bridges [that] open the door of imagination and understanding to the most profound truths of the Bible."[2] God with us—His presence—is one of the most profound realities Scripture shows, teaching us a way forward even when life doesn't make sense. Both our everyday metaphors and the ones we find in Scripture show us how to get from where we are to where we want to be—fully alive in the presence of God.

God's Presence: Face to Face

How do we experience a presence that seems intangible? I've never heard God audibly speak. I've never interlaced my fingers through His gentle hands. I've never seen Him walk through my front door and sit down for dinner.

But Scripture threads the reality of God's presence through its ancient pages. And often, His presence arrives in metaphor. The power of metaphor lies in how simple, everyday things that we can see and touch help us understand the God we cannot yet see. Metaphors make the presence of God tangible and accessible to us.

Metaphoric language is woven even into the fabric of singular words found in Scripture. Consider the word *presence* in the Old Testament: "The most common Hebrew term for 'presence' is *panim* . . . which is also translated 'face,' implying a close and personal encounter with the Lord," according to Dr. Bryan Beyer.[3] *Panim*, according to the University of Iowa, "appears anthropomorphically to describe the divine presence as in Exodus 33:11, 'The Lord used to speak to Moses face (םינפ) to face (םינפ), as one speaks to a friend,' and idiomatically like in Psalm 4:6 to convey divine 'favor': 'Let the light of your face (ךינפ) shine on us, O Lord.'"[4]

Scripture threads the reality of God's presence through its ancient pages, and often, His presence arrives in metaphor.

Pondering the emotional connotation of this word transforms our understanding of God's presence. Attaching the concrete word *face* with God's presence begins to enliven this reality. Being with God is not simply occupying the same space with Him, as when a teacher calls roll, and you respond to confirm your presence among many others. Being face-to-face with God reorients our minds to the intimacy of His presence, beholding the face of the beloved. This experience of His presence shifts from one of disconnection to profound intimacy.

Can you remember the last time you gazed into someone's eyes for more than a few seconds? Holding someone's gaze is an intimate act, one that has been described as looking into someone's soul. *Discover Magazine* detailed an intriguing "modern artistic experiment," involving an extended period of holding another person's gaze:

> Serbian conceptual artist Marina Abramović sat for hours on end in prolonged eye contact with strangers in the atrium of New York's Museum of Modern Art. The 2010 exhibition, "The Artist Is Present," spanned three months, with individuals waiting hours in line for a chance at an intimate gaze-off with Abramović.
>
> After waiting hours in line for her own encounter, writer Rebecca Taylor described her anticipation this way: "I was afraid: afraid of the judgment implicit in staring, afraid of the silence." And yet, as she settled into a half-hour interaction with the artist, she found a surprising peace. Other participants sat for more than an hour, eyes locked with Abramović. Many of them wept. Others smiled or laughed. Some appeared entranced, as if swept away to some distant place or memory—and later said the exchange changed their life or revealed a love they had never felt before.[5]

Abramović was a stranger to those who sat with her. These strangers probably did not expect to have such strong emotional responses to this experiment. But there is something profound and intimate about being face-to-face. Imagine, then, what might happen to those of us who would look for God's presence, as if gazing into His face, in even the unlikely places of our pain and disillusionment. If mere strangers can be entranced, led to peace, enticed to laughter, or experience a revelation of love by gazing into one another's eye, what then, when we come face-to-face with the presence of a God who knows and loves us intimately?

The Gentle Whisper

Elijah, an Old Testament prophet, encountered the presence of this God on a mountainside. After defeating 450 prophets of Baal, Elijah fled the wrath of Queen Jezebel, perhaps upset by how the victory aftermath was playing out. Rather than celebrating this God-sized win, "Elijah was afraid and ran for his life" and soon after tells God, "I have had enough, LORD" (1 Kings 19:3–4). Forty days later, Elijah retreats to a cave and when asked by God what he's doing there, Elijah, focused on the negative and discouraging aspects of his circumstances, says, "I have been very zealous for the LORD God Almighty. The Israelites have rejected your covenant, torn down your altars, and put your prophets to death with the sword. I am the only one left, and now they are trying to kill me too" (1 Kings 19:10).

Maybe you can identify with Elijah's frustrations over discouraging and overwhelming circumstances. Your health diagnosis has swept away your dreams and ambitions. Or a relationship has created ruptures of grief in your life. Maybe the dream job you landed is turning to ash right before your eyes. Perhaps your caretaking role seems like a never-ending task that keeps you isolated and lonely.

If I could rephrase Elijah's complaint for those who are disillusioned, it might be, *I'm doing all I know to do, all I can with what I've been given, and now this? God, I'm done.* That's at least how I felt staring into the grief of a move, a diagnosis, hospitalizations, and a miscarriage.

God meets Elijah in one of his most painful moments and asks, "What are you doing here, Elijah?" (1 Kings 19:9). Instinctively, I hear these words in a preachy lecture. But what if God's tone was gentle, quiet, and kind, like a whisper? 1 Kings 19:11–13 says:

> The LORD said, "Go out and stand on the mountain in the presence of the LORD, for the LORD is about to pass by." Then a great and powerful wind tore the mountains apart and shattered the rocks before the LORD, but the LORD was not in the wind. After the wind there was an earthquake, but the LORD was not in the earthquake. After the earthquake came a fire, but the LORD was not in the fire. And after the fire came a gentle whisper. When Elijah heard it, he pulled his cloak over his face and went out and stood at the mouth of the cave.

In this well-known passage, Elijah experiences God as a gentle whisper, starkly contrasting the violence of the shattering wind, toppling earthquake, and blazing fire. The still, small voice of God soothes over the destruction that preceded it. The whisper of God asks Elijah again, "What are you doing here, Elijah?" (v. 13). God gently invites Elijah to reconsider his mental map, the one that led him to run far away to this mountainside cave, far away from the life God had called him to.

The whisper waits for Elijah to recognize that God is with him, and godlessness and death will not have the last word. Seemingly stuck in his own narrative about the death and destruction that hound him, Elijah responds with the same complaint as the first time, "Your people are acting godless, and now I'm being hunted down so they can kill me."[6] Acknowledging the real, transformative power of God right there with him seems to have escaped Elijah.

Does it escape us too? How often do we get stuck in our own misconceived narratives? The diagnosis, the fractured relationship, the ash heap of lost opportunity, or the drudgery of the mundane seem like the central plotline being written in our lives. Hopelessness and loneliness become the leading characters in the dramas we never asked to be in.

What, though, did God gently remind Elijah of? The prophet didn't have the whole picture in view, and his weariness was likely skewing his perspective. Elijah, who twice said, "I am the only one left" (vv. 10, 14), stands corrected by God: "Yet I reserve seven thousand in Israel" (v. 18). Through a gentle whisper, God invites Elijah to rewrite the mental map of his grief so that he can see that God, in His infinite gentleness, is with him—even in this unlikely place.[7]

We, too, are invited to experience the nature of God's presence in our hard stories through the metaphor of the gentle whisper.

We, too, are invited to experience the nature of God's presence in our hard stories through the metaphor of the gentle whisper. His presence does not resolve all the frustrations, disappointments, or burdens we have, but He will whisper the fullness of His presence with us in the stories we are living. What if we see the metaphors of Scripture as a gateway into this place where we can meet with God?

If we believe that God is angry or incompetent or uninvolved, our grief will shatter us. But Sarah Clarkson reminds us that "a well-woven narrative can be a way to journey through the brokenness, to traverse and map our sorrow, even to find its borders, rather than merely assent to it."[8] If our mental maps and narratives can be transformed by Scripture's metaphors of God's presence, then we can be led to the green pastures and quiet waters of God's good presence even in our pain.

Though the hard got harder for our family—and even more difficulties would pile up over the next several years—I did find God's presence again by the steady practice of rewriting my mental map and narratives through Scripture's metaphors.

My pain and loss felt isolating. Seemingly everywhere I looked, others were blessed with thriving families. Except us. I felt cut off from God, His goodness, and His presence. But when I encountered the gentle whisper of God in Elijah's story, and began journaling about it, I was desperate to find that same gentleness from God, hear His heart for me and my family in the midst of our difficult circumstances, and be able to experience His presence again too.

As I engaged God's gentle whisper in my journaling, here's what I realized: A whisper implies closeness, intimacy, like the intimacy embedded in the Hebrew word *panim* we looked at earlier. And when I stilled and softened toward God's presence, I could hear His truth: *I am with you even here, Allison.*

If you are feeling far from God's heart and presence, let me lend you a little hope and courage. *He is with you.* Even in the most unlikely places, if you can quiet your heart for just a bit, might you hear His gentle whisper? What if you put pen to page to map your way back to God?

JOURNALING PROMPTS

Prompt 1

Can you describe one of the most unlikely places you've encountered God?

Prompt 2

Ask someone you are close to and trust if they're willing to do an experiment with you. Pick a time frame (five, ten, twenty, or thirty minutes) that you will sit face-to-face with this person and gaze into each other's eyes in the spirit of the art museum experiment described earlier in this chapter. Find a spot where you and your partner can sit comfortably face-to-face. Set the timer for the agreed-upon time frame and then quietly gaze into each other's eyes. Once the timer ends, set a five-minute timer and write about your experience in your journal. You can of course keep writing past the five minutes if you want, but the timer gives you permission to only write for five minutes. Here are some questions you can use to get started with your journal entry:

1. Did you like the experiment or not?

2. What physical responses did you have during the experiment?

3. What emotions did you experience as you gazed into your partner's eyes?

4. Did time seem to pass slowly or quickly during the experiment?

5. What is your takeaway from the experience?

Prompt 3

Close your eyes. Breathe deeply. Allow yourself a few moments of quiet and stillness, where all you hear, all you feel, is your steady inhale and exhale. Ask God to open your imagination to Him.

Imagine a place where you might meet with God. This could be your favorite or familiar place, a real place, or an imagined place. Of utmost importance is that the place you imagine is a place you feel safe. In your mind, bring this place alive to your senses. Pause and really explore each of your senses:

- What do you see?
- What do you smell?
- What do you hear?
- What do you feel?

Have you fully immersed yourself in that place? Is it alive in the imagination of your mind? Be fully present in this place as you wait for God to meet you.

Imagine that in an instant, a great, powerful, turbulent wind begins to whip around you, your hair scattering in a thousand directions. Your hair whips around your face, and your knees tremble just a bit, *but* you are held steadfast.

As the great wind tapers and stills, a tremorous shaking begins and becomes so strong you think the ground might open up, *but* you are secure.

As the ground steadies once more, you see flames licking toward you, and they come so close you have to turn your face away from the heat, *but* you are unscathed.

Then, a pause, a stillness, as you brace for the next overwhelming wave.

And yet, what comes is a gentle and quiet whisper. God is here, meeting you in quiet, in stillness, in tenderness.

It's an invitation, as Stacie Poston says, to "sit face to face with the Father and let Him see you. . . . If grief, let Him share grief with you. If joy, let Him smile back at you."[9] However you are, however you've come, sit with Him and let Him gently minister to you.

The invitation is to stay, for as long as you'd like, in the quiet of your mind and heart and listen to the quiet whisper of God. To experience the fullness of His gentleness.

When you're ready, open your eyes and begin to write about your encounter with the gentle, quiet whisper of God.

CHAPTER 3

The Power of Journaling: *Our Mirrors Matter*

To say that I am made in the image of God is to say that love is the reason for my existence, for God is love.

~Thomas Merton

If I could go back a decade, I'd tell myself to look for God in those very unlikely places of a stillbirth, diagnosis, and a miscarriage. Like Elijah finding God in the unexpected gentle whisper. But pain and disappointment can be very disorienting, making it difficult to lift our eyes to the One who is our help.

Pain seems to obscure our holy imagination for what God is doing right in the midst of our most difficult moments.

If I could come to you in your pain, I'd say, "Look, look, He is here! God is here in this pain, in this disappointment, in this disquiet and chaos. He is here!" But I know because I've been there—pain seems to obscure our holy imagination for what God is doing right in the midst of our most difficult moments.

I was stuck with this on repeat in my mind: *If God could not be trusted to get our story right, then He sure couldn't be trusted to help us figure out our new reality.* If He was omnipotent like I'd believed my whole life, then He was choosing not to intervene in our lives, and I couldn't make sense of that.

The ways in which I'd seen the goodness and kindness of God reflected in my life were broken and cracked by pain and confusion.

The Deception of Self-Sufficiency

If God wasn't going to change our circumstances, I would do it myself. My scraped, raw soul tried to latch onto any shard of earthly hope I could grasp to make my life normal again. Therapy and appointments and evaluations and late-night Google searches and alternative medicine became my work and my distraction, my way to numb the pain eating away at me. Honestly, as much as I was motivated to help Reed, I was trying to find my way out of a life I didn't ask for.

That self-sufficiency was an all too familiar habit and way of operating. I had, like so many of us, been raised on the all-American, bootstrapping, individualistic mentality. Alissa Quartz defines this mentality as "getting ahead on only your energy and steam, without help from your family, government, or community. . . . [an] embrace of an individualism that shades into a brittle self-sufficiency."[1] Tim Keller emphasizes how "American culture elevates the interests of the individual over those of family, community, and nation."[2] The cultural waters we are steeped in, without a sufficient and compelling counterbalance, skew our perceptions of how life ought to work.

We see material success and ease of life as an obvious sign of God's blessing, and anything short of that as a personal downfall. We find it easier to slip into and out of church services in darkened rooms rather than show up in love in the real lives of the people in our neighborhoods. We shy away awkwardly from those who are grieving or less than, even though it's a clear call Jesus gives us again and again in the New Testament. We often leave people with pat answers and generic pats on the back of "Let me know if you need anything" when difficulty and grief become part of their living reality. We leave people to sort out their pain and grief on their own. That's the American way, isn't it?

But what do we do when our lives look nothing like the picture of success that's reinforced in every advertisement, sometimes even our churches, and waters the very root of culture's values? What do we do when our lives look nothing like what we've come to believe means we are good and blessed? Too many of us turn to self-sufficiency.

When Reed was two and a half years old, we welcomed our second child, Lucas, into our family, and I was still in the thick of my own delusions about self-sufficiency. As Lucas grew into a toddler and started testing out his newfound independence, he'd proudly stick out his chest and declare to me, "Mom, I do that all by on my own." His cute, determined words made us laugh. Putting on his socks, buckling his car seat harness, and serving himself food at the dinner table? He did not want my help with any of it. But also? His words forced me to look in a mirror at someone whose reflection I didn't want to see.

The logic of "all by on my own" was my mantra as I scheduled appointments, completed physical therapy exercises at home with Reed, and checked things off my to-do list for helping my son overcome his obstacles. While this initially felt productive, I soon realized that Reed wasn't progressing as much as I thought all my effort deserved, and life still felt unbearably hard. Hopelessness settled in. My cycle became to work hard until I crashed; then work harder, and ultimately, crash harder. With each iteration, my heart became more brittle, widening the distance between me in my self-sufficiency and God.

The harder I worked and the harder I crashed, the more the grief intensified. I looked in the mirror and saw a woman who wasn't good enough in the world's eyes to help my son overcome his diagnosis, and wasn't good enough to pull myself out of the despair and crippling depression I felt. My self-sufficiency became the way I tried to prove to God and everyone that I could do this, I could make it, *all by on my own*.

Like the newborn baby I described in chapter 1, I was abruptly pushed into a new, unknown world, rife with disappointments, unknowns, and mounting question marks. As I struggled to live in this new skin I inhabited, the lie of self-sufficiency became the glue I tried to use to hold myself together. Instead of *I can do anything through Christ who strengthens me*, I believed *I can work my own way out of any pain I experience.* When that didn't work, I believed the lie that I had no worth, my son was broken, and I was unloved by God. Instead of allowing the truth that *God would grant me sufficiency for the joy of raising Reed*, I believed that achieving a good life for our family depended solely on my efforts.

Mirrors Matter

My mirror of self-sufficiency was a broken distortion of reality. When the work of metaphor is to translate and hold space between what has been and what is becoming, the accuracy and the truth of the metaphor matters. In this season, the mirror reflected *unworthy*, *broken*, and *unloved*, translating lies instead of truth into my heart and crushing the connection between my heart and God's.

As our daily life with Reed's diagnosis increasingly revolved around reminders that my child was atypical, I started to believe more and more that I *had* to fix him because the world would never make a place for him unless I did. I convinced myself that I must work as hard as I could to mend what was broken. The self-sufficiency reflected in culture was only a bid for control that led to deeper grief and brokenness because none of us are designed to bear the weight of authoring our own stories.

> When the work of metaphor is to translate and hold space between what has been and what is becoming, the accuracy and the truth of the metaphor matters.

Self-sufficiency seems like the golden ticket to success, to the life we've always dreamed of. While God has imbued us with agency and choice, ultimately, much lies outside our grasp for control. We think doing it ourselves is the formula for getting the life we want. It's the old Edenic lie that when we're in control, when we make the decisions, when we get what we want, then all will be right in our lives. Our hearts will finally be satisfied.

Or so we think.

In our limited knowledge and wisdom as finite beings, I'm not sure we'd make the best decisions even if we had total control of our lives. Control ultimately wouldn't serve us well because our decisions would be self-serving at best and self-destructive at worst.

And yet, we often live our lives bent on wrestling control away from God. We want control. But God wants a relationship. In relationship with God, we can make sense out of the pain and brokenness of our lives. In relationship with God, we can trace the lines of grace that He's weaving into our stories and find life abundant.

This cultural obsession with self-sufficiency, individualism, and success clashes head-on, of course, with Scripture, which provides the over-abundant, compelling counternarrative to this destructive, out-of-balance mindset and soul posture. Paul reminds us in 2 Corinthians 3:5: "Not that we are sufficient in ourselves to claim anything as coming from us, but our sufficiency is from God" (ESV). As Pete Briscoe aptly points out, "*We are not called to live super-human lives through our own hidden powers.* We are designed to live in dependence on God. When we are weak, He is strong. When we are foolish, He is wise. When we don't know what to say, He gives us the words."[3]

But this shift won't happen magically. If it did, most of us would already have this figured out. What we need is a tool, a practice, a discipline for reorienting us away from our delusion of self-sufficiency and toward a healed, whole relationship with the God of the universe.

A Different Mirror

I was at the beginning of the long, often painful, but ultimately beautiful journey of replacing self-sufficiency with lament, depth, long-suffering, love, openness, and vulnerability. It would not happen immediately or even in a linear fashion.

Just like I needed new skin to live in after being thrust into a post-diagnosis life, I also needed a new mirror that would reflect *beloved of God*, *whole in Christ*, and *worthy of all of God's good gifts.* I needed the mirror of 1 Corinthians 13:

> If I speak in the tongues of men or of angels, but do not have love, I am only a resounding gong or clanging cymbal. If I have the gift of prophecy and can fathom all mysteries and all knowledge, and if I have a faith that can move mountains, but do not have love, I am nothing. If I give all I possess to the poor and give over my body to hardship that I may boast, but do not have love, I gain nothing.
>
> Love is patient, love is kind. It does not envy, it does not boast, it is not proud. It does not dishonor others, it is not self-seeking, it is not easily angered, it keeps no record of wrongs. Love does not delight in evil but rejoices with the truth. It always protects, always trusts, always hopes, always perseveres. (vv. 13:1–7)

In this passage threaded with metaphor, Paul makes love the priority, the ultimate good, the highest value. The make-it-or-break-it necessity. Without love, we are nothing, Paul says. The starkness of his language is intentional because the importance of love cannot be overstated. As the Message conveys this truth,

“No matter what I say, what I believe, and what I do, I’m bankrupt without love” (1 Cor. 13:3–7).

Paul personifies love. He makes this abstract quality tangible so we can see who love is. This, he seems to be saying, is love with skin on. When we look into the mirror of God’s love, we see patience, kindness, humility, deference, delight in truth, protection, trust, hope, and perseverance. In contrast, self-sufficiency looked like self-first entitlement to my own desires, ruminating on all that was wrong rather than all that was good, and boasting in my own efforts and what I could do all on my own. Self-sufficiency protected me without regard for others. I did not trust anyone, not even God, and was filled with despair. My self-sufficiency ultimately brought me to nothing.

Self-sufficiency became the grit and grime that obscured the mirror of love God was inviting me to look in to. The self-sufficiency became a distraction from how desperately I needed to know that Reed’s diagnosis wasn’t a punishment and that God still loved me. Looking back a few years later, what I would see is how patiently and kindly God loved me through all my clamoring and clanging attempts to right our story.

The mirrors we choose to look in to, to reflect back truth to us, matter so much because “for now we see only a reflection as in a mirror” (1 Cor. 13:12). On this side of eternity, we only have mirrors to see and understand our realities, and the wrong mirror distorts the truth and will eventually shatter us. But there is a day coming when “we shall see face to face” (1 Cor. 13:12), and love will not be just a reflection but a real, lived experience in the presence of Love Himself.

Looking through God’s mirror of love, we will not be crushed in the midst of diagnoses. Our unloveliness, our not enough-ness, our misunderstandings are transformed when viewed through the mirror of God's strong, wise, Word-made-flesh love. Like mine was, is your mirror distorted? Are you gazing through the smoke and mirrors of the enemy's lies? If so, what you need is God's clear mirror of love and all-sufficiency.

Journaling can be a way to hold up the mirror of God's love, a mirror that helps us trace the lines of God's good grace in our lives. Without reflection, we become "like someone who looks at his face in a mirror and, after looking at himself, goes away and immediately forgets what he looks like. But whoever looks intently into the perfect law that gives freedom, and continues in it—not forgetting what they have heard, but doing it—they will be blessed in what they do" (James 1:23–25).

What is this perfect law? "'Love the Lord your God with all your heart and with all your soul and with all your mind and with all your strength.' The second is this: 'Love your neighbor as yourself'" (Mark 12:30–31). Journaling is one practice that helps us live out this command. When we process our emotions through journaling, we engage our heart. When we listen for the still, small whisper of God as we journal, we engage our souls.

Journaling is one practice that helps us live out the command to love the Lord with all our heart, soul, mind, and strength.

When we write, we neurologically engage our minds. According to the University of Waterloo, "Writing is an extraordinary process that requires a complex interplay of many brain regions. . . . the frontal lobe, hippocampus, Broca's area, Wernicke's area, visual cortex, motor area and the caudate nucleus."[4] According to Adam Young, "If you are able to tell your story while remaining connected to your emotions, then the neural networks in the left part of your brain will link up with the neural networks in the right part of your brain. This is very healing. It leads to what neuroscientists call integration, and what the Bible calls shalom."[5]

As I began to journal about our experience with Reed, I noticed that the heaviness was lifting, even if just a bit, and I could take a breath. I began to see new ways of thinking and being that I never would have seen apart from them staring back at me from the pages of my journal. My journal became a mirror, reflecting to me God's truth, wisdom, and love. Because writing it all down helped, I continued, page after page, as honestly as I could. At the time I only knew that journaling was balm for my soul. Writing through my pain was healing me, and I needed as much of it as I could get.

There is a reason why writing through our pain is healing. Adam Young says it most simply and profoundly: "It turns out that the practice of reflecting on the story of your life actually promotes healing in your brain . . . [because] brain health is a function of the degree to which all parts of your brain are connected with one another."[6]

Young goes on to point out that sharing our stories with others is also crucial for brain healing. Journaling can be the first reflective step toward this healing, especially if the idea of sharing our story out loud with someone else is slightly (or majorly) terrifying. Engaging our stories on the safe pages of our journals, just between us and God, is a safe, important first step. Journaling communities can complete the other half of Young's puzzle, and we'll talk more about journaling in community in chapter 7.

In the hurried, demanding lives we lead, we spend most of our thoughts on the to-do lists just to get us through our days, sprinkled in with the same, looping thoughts of regret, frustration, and the nagging thought of things we know we need to do but just can't remember. If we're going to heal our relationships with God and find hope, we've got to dig beneath that conscious clutter to find out what thoughts, ideas, and feelings are a distorted reflection of reality and God's love.

Journaling can help us honestly examine the ways we're navigating our stories, which is important for growth. Before we can change or grow, we need to see the truth of our circumstances, our perspectives, and our connection to God. Journaling functions as this mirror where we put in plain view for ourselves the patterns of our thoughts. And, then, when we journal God's honest truth back to ourselves, we make visible the often invisible, intangible work of the Spirit in us.

When we journal God's honest truth back to ourselves, we make visible the often invisible, intangible work of the Spirit in us.

Dr. James Pennebaker developed and studied a four-day journal writing protocol, which he outlines in his book *Writing to Heal: A Guided Journal for Recovering from Trauma and Upheaval.* Each day, for fifteen to twenty minutes per day, participants would write about a personally and emotionally difficult topic, guided by simple prompts that helped them explore their stories, connect their story to the greater scope of their lives, and ultimately find their voice within their stories. After the four-day protocol, participants showed improvement in physical health, emotional well-being, reduced visits to doctors, and improved immune systems.[7]

Similar to Pennebaker's participants, I found that journaling was helping me heal from the destructive nature of self-sufficiency. I began to see that what I really needed wasn't control but the ability to create meaning and insight from my story, which journaling is so helpful for doing.

It turned out that what Reed really needed, even more than the therapies and interventions, was radical acceptance born from love. God was already looking at my son, at our family, and the life He'd given us and saying it was good. I didn't have to fight for the good life; *I already had it.*

In truth, what *I* needed was to learn the art of radical acceptance of this new path God had us on. I needed to see that even in my immense suffering, that the very good things of God—faith, hope, and love—were reflected even more clearly. I'd just been looking in the wrong mirror.

JOURNAL PROMPTS

Prompt 1

Hold the mirror up of these verses from Scripture and the following quote from Anne Lindbergh to your current pain or difficulty. How do these words help you see or understand your pain differently?

1. "But the fruit of the Spirit is love, joy, peace, forbearance, kindness, goodness, faithfulness, gentleness and self-control. Against such things there is no law" (Gal. 5:22–23).
2. "I do not believe that sheer suffering teaches. If suffering alone taught, all the world would be wise, since everyone suffers. To suffering must be added mourning, understanding, patience, love, openness, and the willingness to remain vulnerable."[8]

Prompt 2

Like my realization about self-sufficiency, can you remember a time when someone held up a metaphorical mirror to your life that helped you see things differently? Set a five-minute timer and write about that experience.

Prompt 3

Close your eyes. Breathe deeply. Allow yourself a few moments of quiet and stillness, where all you hear, all you feel, is your steady inhale and exhale. Ask God to open your imagination to Him.

Sit in front of a mirror for three to five minutes. As you see yourself in the mirror, what comes to mind? Write down whatever comes to mind without censoring your thoughts.

Take a pause and then write down several truths about how God sees you. Possible Scripture verses to look at: 1 Samuel 16:7, 1 John 3:1, 1 Peter 2:9, 2 Corinthians 5:17, Psalm 139:13–16, Matthew 5:14, and Colossians 3:12.

After reading those truths several times through (consider writing down and taping those truths to the mirror), look back at yourself in the mirror. What comes to mind as you see yourself with God's truth reflected back? How does God's truth help shift your inner narrative? Spend some time in your journal writing those answers down.

CHAPTER 4

The Potency of Journaling and Metaphor:

Burying Seeds

Judge each day not by the harvest you reap but by the seeds you plant.

~William A. Ward

After five years in Pennsylvania, our now family of five moved back to my home state of South Carolina. We were depleted emotionally, vocationally, and financially. We lost substantial income, gained an embarrassing amount of debt, saw the seams of our family fracture, and otherwise qualified as failed at life. I spiraled into depression, no longer able to cope under the weight of our grief and circumstances.[1]

Did we have solid jobs lined up? No. Did we know how five of us would live in a small, two-bedroom condo that waited for us back home? No. But we were desperate to be back near family (and warmer weather) as we continued to raise our young family and navigate the challenges of raising a son with special needs.

The plan was for Ben to run his own marketing business and for me to focus my time and efforts on being mama to our three small children—Reed who was six, Lucas who was three, and our daughter, Ansley, who was almost a year old.

Ben's marketing business struggled to get off the ground. To fill the gaps this left in our budget, Ben began doing handyman work on the side. Now he was running two businesses and working nonstop. No matter how hard or how long he worked, money seemed to run like water through a sieve.

I was growing bitter over being home alone all the time and feeling unsupported. I was still shouldering years of unprocessed, accumulated, compounded grief from my niece's stillbirth, the move to Pennsylvania (and back), and Reed's diagnosis. Piled on top of that was adjusting to not teaching college writing courses, something I'd done (and loved) for more than a decade.

Then, Ben confessed a soul-damaging secret he'd kept hidden for a year. He had emotionally checked out of our relationship and turned to the old, destructive, escapist habit of viewing pornography. His breach of trust stunned me.

My heart only felt numb, with no capacity to feel one more terrible thing. Sometimes, the numbness would wear off just a bit and the swirling river of grief would rush out as anger over seemingly small, inconsequential decisions, like whether to upgrade to a new phone.

One night, after working long hours as usual, Ben came through the front door of our 1,000 square foot condo with a shiny plastic bag in his hand.

At the lowest of low points, Satan's lies are easy to believe.

"What's that?" I asked, with one eyebrow cocked.

"Oh, I upgraded to the new iPhone today," he nonchalantly replied.

While our finances are in shambles? Without asking me? Because he thought he deserved it? Without upgrading mine?

Questions shot through my mind like barbed wire, ripping my mind and heart apart with anger, hurt, and self-righteous indignation. This seemingly small transgression felt like the final stroke that took our story beyond grace and redemption's reach.

At the lowest of low points, Satan's lies were easy to believe. *I was alone. Our lives were ruined. Grace wouldn't reach us here.* We argued a bit that night about the phone, but the tiredness I felt in my bones, the anger that had worn me down to a nub, the hopelessness that sifted through the holes in my heart, left me with no more energy to care.

I was buried in a deep hole of depression.

Standing at our sliding back door, I watched my children play chase in the backyard with our neighbor's little boy. My shoulders sagged under the weight of the impossibility of our life.

My children's play was light and free-spirited, and their smiles were joyful. My eyes squinted against the sharpness of the midafternoon summer sun bouncing off the tops of their hair. They chased and tumbled after each other, shrieking and giggling with delight when they'd tag someone else who now had to be "it." I felt detached, unable to muster a smile at their play.

I'm pretty sure they'd be better off without me.

For the first time in many long months, all other thoughts went quiet in my mind, as if someone had turned off every light, except this one terrible, illuminated thought. The sight of my children playing in the backyard faded from my eyes, and I gawked at the intrusive, nine-word statement hanging awkwardly in my mind as the quiet, inviting darkness saturated my mind.

I blinked slowly, almost frozen. As quickly as the thought entered my mind, another one whispered: *That's not from God.*

I stared down a road divided: One path was dark and hopeless, haunted by failures, the enemy's lies, and my own disappointment. The other path—lined with a good God, a compassionate therapist, and a community of people who loved me—was illuminated with life.[2]

In an instant, I saw the fight between life and death. I could either wake up and embrace the story God was writing in my family, or I would continue to bury myself in the depths of despair, depression, and death. The kind of emotional death that suffocates you. The kind of spiritual death that hollows you out like a wasteland.

In this moment of clarity and decision I knew nothing would ever be the same again.

I was faced with the same rebuke that Moses gave to the Israelites:

> "This day I call the heavens and the earth as witnesses against you that I have set before you life and death, blessings and curses. Now choose life, so that you and your children may live and that you may

> love the Lord your God, listen to his voice, and hold fast to him. For the Lord is your life, and he will give you many years in the land he swore to give to your fathers, Abraham, Isaac and Jacob." (Deut. 30:19–20)

Really, at the heart of my struggles was the inability to look at the life God had given me and see good—or even the possibility that God could bring any good out of it. I couldn't look at my son and his disability and call it good. I couldn't look at the relational fractures in my life and call it good. I couldn't look at our financial upending and call it good. I couldn't look at the reckoning moment in my marriage and call it good. Who in their right mind *would* call any of those losses good?

Only in the upside-down, inside-out way of God's kingdom could good come *from* these terrible things. Because God is all goodness and light, He wasn't expecting me to call all this brokenness good.

But each of those devastations was an invitation from God to go deeper with Him, to find His goodness in the midst of the pain. To know, like Joseph, that what otherwise might have been intended for evil, "God intended it for good to accomplish what is now being done, the saving of many lives" (Gen. 50:20). If I believed that God created my son, then I had to believe that his story—our family's story—could, in God's grace, be rewritten into a good story. That, as Jesus proclaims in the Beatitudes, in our mourning, we would be comforted. That I could find life not despite our losses, but because of them. That God was doing something good in the midst of this wildly difficult story.

When Death Brings Life

Real life only comes from death. Jesus said, "Unless a kernel of wheat falls to the ground and dies, it remains only a single seed. But if it dies, it produces many seeds" (John 12:24). Unless I could let my old life with its dreams and hopes die, bury all of it in the ground of faith, and trust that God would resurrect a new life for my family, then I would never live again.

> When we know that God is with us in the crucible, we can keep putting one foot in front of the other.

I'm struck by Jesus' use of the wheat metaphor, not only because it's something His listeners would understand but also because it reinforces the paradox of the gospel. Somewhere along the way, I had come to expect an easy, smooth life free of obstacles, loss, or pain. When that picture crumbled, I wanted out. I wanted deliverance from the very aspect of my life that God had good plans for.

Whether it's the death of a person, the death of a dream, or the death of a relationship, when we can see that death births life and serves a greater purpose, healing becomes possible. And when we know that God is with us in the crucible, we can keep putting one foot in front of the other.

That moment staring out of the back door was the catalyst, my wake-up call to choose life or death. I wanted to choose life. But how would I forge a way forward?

God was inviting me to take the seeds of my life and plant them in the ground, to bury what was, let it disappear beneath the dirt, and let the pebbles and roots rearrange to accommodate new life. I could only pray that the Good Farmer would help me trust His wise, weathered hands, to keep these seeds in trust.[3]

John 12:25–28 says, "Anyone who loves their life will lose it, while anyone who hates their life in this world will keep it for eternal life. Whoever serves me must follow me; and where I am, my servant also will be. My Father will honor the one who serves me. *Now my soul is troubled, and what shall I say?* 'Father, save me from this hour'? No, it was for this very reason I came to this hour. Father, glorify your name!'"

I could only forge a way forward by following Jesus, who acknowledged the very real pain of the path marked out for Him. He plainly states that His soul was troubled. No whitewashed platitudes. No trite clichés or pats on the back. Just a real, honest confession.

In contrast, I think about the disciples after His crucifixion, trying to process the inconceivable loss of their leader, teacher, mentor, friend, and brother. Did they try to comfort themselves with the same platitudes we often resort to? You know, the phrases that start with the cringe-worthy, *"At least His suffering is over," "He's with so-and-so in heaven," or "We have good memories of Him." "You know, It could have been worse."*

Or were they able to look at their bewildering situation, and like the wandering Israelites, ask of the manna, "What is it?" (Ex. 16:15). Could they own their disappointment, heartbreak, incredulity, the very real sense that maybe God got this ending wrong? Call it what it was instead of airbrushing it with some silver-lining pseudo-gospel? Give up the fool's gold as they wrestled with this harrowing plot twist?

Jesus was God in our likeness, in the substance of a human. And in His humanness, how did Jesus suffer the crucifixion? Beforehand in the garden, He acknowledged the agony of accepting this as God's best answer. He wept, became physically undone. He didn't say, "*Well, at least I know how this all turns out.*"

Is it possible that if we refuse the fool's gold of a silver lining, then we can revel in the glorious reality of resurrection? Only then, perhaps, will the life-giving power of resurrection bind us up, hold us together, and hold us in awe when life gets turned upside down.

With Reed's diagnosis, my life was marked by *before* diagnosis and *after* diagnosis. The person I'd been, the mom I'd expected to be, the son I thought I'd have, died. I wasn't sure I wanted to be alive in this new, bewildering life. Some well-meaning people told us, *"You're the perfect parents for him,"* or *"At least he has his daddy's red hair,"* and *"Oh, he's just fine the way he is."* None of those sentiments really helped when my story went so unbearably off course.

Could our life bloom in this desert? Instead of a silver lining, could we see true, resplendent glory? Would we find that God was piecing us back together? Whole again but reformed. Reshaped. Remade. More in His image. Could we know that He looked at us, at our boy, and said we are *good*?[4]

Yes, Jesus acknowledges His pain, and in His most harrowing hour, also says, "Not my will, but yours be done" (Luke 22:42). I didn't need my old life back or for Reed's disorder to miraculously disappear. I didn't need a way out of my own Gethsemane. I needed to die to myself and to say with my whole heart, mind, soul, and might: "Not my will with my family, God, but Yours."

Pat Schneider, in her book *How the Light Gets In*, muses that "the *open sesame* into writing is almost always a concrete image,"[5] which forms the substance of all metaphors. Even research supports the effectiveness of using metaphors to improve our mental and emotional health. In one journaling study Jarrett, participants were directed "to be either literal, 'I felt anxious or confused,' or metaphorical: 'I felt like a leaf in the wind.'"[6] Guess which group of participants experienced improvement with depression and negative emotions? Only the ones who wrote through metaphors.

When life has dealt us a difficult blow or confusing circumstances, journaling through metaphors offers us an open door toward growth and healing. When our minds shut down or our pens refuse to move across the page, metaphors can nudge our minds open and our pens across the page because they give us a familiar framework of understanding. Journaling through metaphors can beautifully transform our old neural maps and ways of thinking by letting in just enough light to trace the lines of grace through them.

Journaling through metaphors can beautifully transform our old ways of thinking by letting in just enough light to trace the lines of grace through them.

So, to fight back death and darkness, I picked up my pen and began choosing life with the words I scrawled out in my journal and with the Word Himself.

I had to learn to acknowledge that, yes, my life had irrevocably changed, but I also needed to have faith that beauty was on the horizon, that our story wasn't finished, and we would see the goodness of the Lord again.

When our lives get turned upside down, it's often hard to see the small graces that whisper restoration is coming. In retrospect, I can see that Ben's confession, while brutally painful, was the doorway to repentance and healing. What if he hadn't confessed his wrongdoing? Maybe that secret would have been our undoing. What if I had never been startled awake by the terrible thought that my family might be better off without me? Maybe I would have succumbed to the darkness.

Small graces can begin to put cracks in the lies that threaten to undo us, and these cracks create just enough room so the Light can begin to peek through. With a bit of light and the smallest seed of faith, our stories that started in death can be resurrected in God's goodness.

JOURNAL PROMPTS

Prompt 1

Make a list of the "nothing will be the same after this" moments. These are moments where your life path has shifted, in a way that you know everything has changed.

Prompt 2

Next to the hard moments you listed in #1, write one word that represents the good God brought from what otherwise might have been meant for evil. If you still feel in the dark about the good God is bringing from some of the items on your list, write the word "seed" next to those as a reminder of faith that you are trusting God to bring good from that very thing.

Prompt 3

Close your eyes. Breathe deeply. Allow yourself a few moments of quiet and stillness, where all you hear, all you feel, is your steady inhale and exhale. Ask God to open your imagination to Him.

Before you begin journaling this next prompt, look back over the list you created for the first prompt. Choose one of the items from your list, perhaps one that has "seed" written next to it, and write that item at the top of a blank page. Then,

I want you to close your eyes for a few moments and imagine that in the palm of your hand, you hold a small seed. This seed represents the word or phrase you chose from your list. Allow your breathing to deepen and slow so as to invite quiet stillness into this moment. Inhale and exhale deeply and slowly six to eight times. Allow yourself to consider the seed in your hand.

- What is difficult about that seed?
- What about the seed do you not want to release?

When you're ready, envision gently pushing that seed into the ground. Releasing it to the care of the Good Shepherd. Trusting that He will take this act of faith and in letting go, in the dying of this thing, new life will come to be. Abundant, multiplying resurrection will come from this release. Acknowledge any pain that comes as you release this seed to God.

Then, imagine placing your hand flat atop the ground and asking the Good Farmer to help you trust His wise, weathered hands to keep these seeds in trust. Remind yourself that as you yield, He will bring the yield. Lay this seed in trust and possibility. When you're ready, journal your experience of releasing your seed and trusting God for resurrection.

CHAPTER 5

Light as Metaphor:

Seeing the Goodness of God

In the heart of the earth, in the human heart, in the heart of the mystery, darkness and light are inextricably bound together.

~Pat Schneider

Pain became a pathway into God's goodness and life.

But most of us turn *away from* instead of *into* our pain. That's certainly what I did for the decade following Reed's diagnosis. First, I was numb. Then I was angry.

Then I turned toward self-sufficient productivity, which ultimately turned to brokenness and despair. As Dr. Denise Fornier says, "We aren't wrong for wanting to avoid feeling pain. It's a perfectly human, perfectly natural thing to do. It just turns out to be ineffective."[1]

What if instead I had turned toward my pain? Allowed it to move through me? Met it with compassion and curiosity rather than fear and apprehension? Sought Jesus in it rather than turning from Him?

What if you, too, could allow your pain to open up new pathways for grace?

Our natural, human inclination may be to turn away from our pain, fearful that we are cracking wide open. If we can pay close enough attention, though, we learn the true narrative. The cracks aren't disassembling us. They are breaking open deep wells of grace and light, if only we have the vision to see it.[2]

My journey back to wholeness began by acknowledging my pain, and it started with one step, one counseling appointment, one medication, one conversation, one journal entry at a time. The daily in and out of this journey was anything but neat, tidy, and linear. In fact, excruciating might be more accurate. There were days I was not sure I would be whole again.

Months later, Dane Ortlund's words would show me that what had kept me trapped by death was what I had failed to see. I couldn't see that my own sadness "was endured by [Jesus] in the past and [was also] shouldered by him"[3] in that season of suffering. Jesus' presence was the goodness I couldn't perceive.

Ortlund's words reminded me that Jesus' heart, His very nature, compelled Him to be with me in my pain and bear the weight of my deep darkness. Pain had crowded out my vision. I closed my eyes, and this time saw myself sitting, head bent and cradled between my knees, feeling the palpable sadness and gritty reality of the darkness that had been enveloping me.

But then, I pictured Jesus. Sitting close to me, holding off the darkness. I sensed the tangible reality of His love pushing out the darkness and enveloping me. I saw that even in my depression, He had been sustaining me with His presence. For that moment, the veil between heaven and earth became a thin space, and that moment became the beginning of my healing.[4]

The Power of Poetry

To become a student of turning toward our pain, I can think of no better place to turn than the Psalms. The artistry and poetry of the Psalms paint brilliant, beautiful pictures of gospel paradox. In their words, we find lament, hope, despair, joy, anger, praise, questions, and sometimes, all of them intertwined in the same psalm. The word pictures created in the Psalms—the poetry of the Bible—become some of the best case studies for metaphor. Phyllis Klein says, "Poetry gives rhythm to silence, light to darkness. In poetry, we find the magic of metaphor, compactness of expression, use of the five senses, and simplicity or complexity of meaning in a few lines."[5]

The word pictures created in the Psalms become some of the best-case studies for metaphor.

In fact, according to Quina Aragon:

> A good third of God's Word is poetry. God inspired Adam toward poetry when He gave him Eve. God taught and warned His people by teaching Moses a song. Job expressed his unfathomable suffering through poetry, and God spoke back likewise. The prophets often said, "Thus says the Lord," and out came poetry. And then there's the

> book of Psalms. God taught His covenant people to write their sorrows, their joys, their fears, their longings in poetry for them to sing to Him again and again and again.[6]

What I've found is that the poetry of the Psalms can "midwife" us through our pain and into the goodness and presence of God when we let their rhythm and silence, light and darkness, and their juxtaposed metaphors and words work through us in our writing. While simply reading the Psalms can be powerful in and of itself, journaling with the Psalms helps us even more actively engage in the process of the renewal and transformation of our minds.

Journaling is one of the most powerful practices we can engage in to live in the reality of God's good light. According to Dr. Abbey Houde, "your brain possesses remarkable adaptability, yet it often defaults to familiar patterns. To truly transform it, simply shifting your thoughts isn't enough—you must engage in practices that actively reshape it: [like] journal[ing]."[7] If we want to move through and transform our pain, we actually have to do something—like journaling—to do so. Like we discussed in chapter 2, journaling helps us create a map, a path, through our pain and back to God. We must, however, become adept mapmakers.

A Psalm in Real Life

My niece Zoey's death had brought me to the turbulent waters of immense, life-altering loss. Weeks after my niece's stillbirth, in a haze of grief, I stumbled across Psalm 27:13: "I remain confident of this: I will see the goodness of the LORD in the land of the living." Our family was walking through the valley of the shadow of death, and David's confidence seemed jarring to me. His words and his confidence in God's goodness angered me, honestly. He was no stranger to grief, and yet he adamantly believed in God's goodness. I wondered how God could be good when He seemingly ripped an answered prayer right out from under my family. I wondered how God could be good when some babies never take a breath outside of the womb.

And yet, in the midst of David's chaos, he claimed God's goodness. Scholars believe that David wrote Psalm 27 fleeing either his power-hungry son Absalom or the tempestuous King Saul. How could he have this kind of confidence while running for his very life?

In my journal, I copied down Psalm 27:13, reading and rereading the verse written across the page, trying to make sense of the paradox. What I felt seemed miles apart from the verse that was plainly written out in front of me. *God*, I wrote in my journal, *how? How can anyone have confidence in Your goodness when our hearts are torn apart?* The question sat taut in my heart. In the lingering silence, the Holy Spirit gently reminded me of the mustard seed. All I needed was a mustard-sized seed of faith that God would shelter me in His mercy as I walked this path of grief and to trust that even if I didn't feel it yet, confidence in the goodness of the Lord would come.

With time and retrospect, Zoey showed me that even in our darkest pain, God is as close as the oxygen in our lungs. In her death, she birthed new life into our family, in the paradoxical way that only grace can. If we'd have written the story, surely, we'd have kept her here. But in the absence of that, we pressed into her story to see Jesus. To be filled with grace. To love more earnestly.[8] Whoever knew such good gifts could come out of such heart-rending loss?

Psalm 27: God's Presence

Metaphors, like the ones we see in Psalm 27, can surprise us with their shocking intertwining of courage and joy in the midst of harrowing circumstances. This juxtaposition invites us into real and tangible experience of knowing God and His presence.

The whole of Psalm 27 is predicated on being in God's presence and focusing our hearts on the beauty we behold there. David asks to dwell in God's house, to gaze on God's beauty, and to seek God in His temple. David is confident that God will keep him safe and shelter him. Meditating on these truths draws David to declare that his head will be lifted up and he will offer God a sacrifice with loud joy, and that he will sing and make music to God. Remember, David is declaring this in the midst of running for his life.

God outside of time is not hurried or rushed. He has all the time in the world for us.

I can't help but think of Marina Abramović's countercultural, experimental exhibit, "The Artist Is Present," we talked about in chapter 2. She invited total strangers to experience a fully present presence. The God of the whole universe invites us to be in His presence, not because we are strangers, but because He loves us intimately. God outside of time is not hurried or rushed. In His infinite capacity, He has all the time in the world for us. His presence is all-encompassing. The beauty is unending. The question is, in the midst of our pain and disappointment, will we pause and accept His invitation? Will we taste and see that the Lord is good?

Psalm 27: Light as Metaphor

The very first verse of Psalm 27 gives us one of the first metaphors, which focuses on God as light. David is borrowing the language of something tangible (light) to describe something less tangible (God).

What does light illuminate about God? When darkness and difficulty surround David, God is his refuge and Savior. *Merriam-Webster* defines light as "something that makes vision possible."[9] This metaphor of light relies on our common experience of light as safety. This metaphor works to help us understand how even in the midst of terrifying difficulty we can still be safe.

Were you like me as a young child, absolutely terrified of the dark? Standing at the end of our darkened hallway, the same one I'd walked thousands of times in my childhood in broad daylight, and yet at night, I could not inch my way forward, convinced some scary monster was waiting to devour me. Every night, I insisted that my parents leave the hallway light on so that I would not be in total darkness. Turn one small light on, and my anxiety would wash out like the tide. I could walk confidently down the hallway. I could fall asleep peacefully and without hesitation. Light makes us feel safe. Nothing had changed about this hallway—nothing except my ability to see accurately.

When David recognizes God as his light, nothing about his circumstances changed; he was still running for his life after all. But everything about his perspective, his ability to see clearly, changed. I had my own light epiphany when I realized Jesus was with me in the darkness of my grief and depression. The crippling struggle that threatened to undo me was rendered impotent by the simple yet astounding reality of Jesus' presence. Jesus with me gave me the vision to see that I was not alone or forsaken.

God is light. In the midst of disorienting circumstances, God makes us feel safe. Like David, God gives us vision to see our circumstances from His perspective, one in which we are safe and protected in Him. While we think we see clearest in broad daylight, we often see God's light, His presence, most clearly from our darkest circumstances. Consider the paradox that in darkness we more easily find the light. In God's light, we are protected from danger and find ourselves in a place of security. Though the externals may be in chaos, our hearts and souls are secure in God.

As an adult, dark hallways don't paralyze me as they used to. Even having lived through my worst fears realized, I still scan the future for threats on the horizon. I wonder and worry, *What if? What if the other shoe drops? What if the next, most terrible thing happens?* There's no limit to the bad that can happen to us. Just ask Job. *What then?*

Then we know that God is with us. We are confident that in His goodness, He is working all things out for our good. We know that He is in the business of resurrection and redemption. We know that we can "taste and see that the Lord is good" (Ps. 34:8). We know that "the Lord God is a sun and shield; the Lord bestows favor and honor; no good thing does he withhold from those whose walk is blameless" (Ps. 84:11). And we can be confident, that in the presence of God's Light, we will, like David, see the goodness of the Lord.

Exodus 3: Another Kind of Light

I think of Moses' encounter with God: "There the angel of the Lord appeared to him in flames of fire from within a bush. Moses saw that though the bush was on fire it did not burn up" (Ex. 3:2). I'm awed by how the bush "did not burn up". Any fire I've ever watched has burned everything in it to ash. But the flames did not consume the bush because God was in it. And from that burning fire, Moses received his calling to shepherd the Israelites out of Egyptian slavery and into their promised land.

God used fire to prepare the way for a new season in Moses' life. As Moses approached the blaze, God told him, "Take off your sandals, for the place where you are standing is holy ground" (Ex. 3:5). Any place God is with us is holy ground. Because He lives in us, our very lives are holy ground. And if that other shoe drops? Well, it drops on holy ground.

"But Moses said to God, 'Who am I that I should go to Pharaoh and bring the Israelites out of Egypt?'" (Ex. 3:11). Moses is reluctant to take this new assignment. His anxiety peeks through the *what-if* question he poses to God: "Suppose I go to the Israelites and say to them, 'The God of your fathers has sent me to you,' and they ask me, 'What is his name?' Then what shall I tell them?" (Ex. 3:13).

We can trust that God is with us, and most of all, that our souls are safe in Him.

God's answer to Moses' anxiety is that He will be with him (Ex. 3:12) and that He is the I Am (Ex. 3:14). Difficulties and unknowns might raise the temperature of our anxiety. Still, we can trust that God is with us, and as the God of the universe, He's working out good things in us through our circumstances. And most of all, our souls are safe in Him.

With the gift of hindsight, I see that in the fire of stillbirth, diagnosis, miscarriage, and personal failures, God was strengthening my heart to trust Him more fully by burning away the thoughts, fears, and feelings disrupting my faith. He is, after all, a consuming fire (Deut. 4:24).

Through fire, in kindness, and with purpose, God is weaving each season of your life together too, each serving its unique purpose and giving way to the next. Whatever each season holds, you can be confident in God's presence leading and guiding you. You can be confident that God has good things for you, even amidst the truly difficult things. You can confidently face whatever each season brings because He is with you. And you and I can let the metaphors in Scripture, the poetry of the Psalms, remind us again and again of all His goodness.

JOURNALING PROMPTS

Prompt 1

Can you think of a time when light in any form (e.g., candle, fireplace, lamp) represented something positive or healing for you? Spend some time writing about that experience. I especially encourage you to write through your five senses as you journal because the work of metaphor is to give tangible skin to the unseen, less tangible aspects of our lives (thoughts, feelings, our inner world). In this experience, you're describing:

- What did you *see*?
- What did you *hear*?
- What did you *taste*?
- What did you *smell*?
- What did you *touch*?

Prompt 2

Want to try your hand at writing a poem? I know some of you will freeze up at this idea. But! Remember. This is your journal, and no one else ever has to see it. I have found that poetry uniquely frees me in my journaling. I feel no pressure in a poem to write a complete sentence or even a connected thought. A poem is incredibly welcoming and accommodating. And, I will teach you a really simple method for writing a poem, one that you may have even done way back in elementary school: an acrostic. For this kind of poem, you pick a phrase to write vertically, one letter at a time, down the page. You can come up with your own phrase or use my suggestion, which is relevant to the focus of this chapter: God Is Light. So, it would look like this down your journal page—

G ______________________

O ______________________

D ______________________

I ______________________

S ______________________

L ______________________

I ______________________

G ______________________

H ______________________

T ______________________

To write the poem, each line will begin with a word that starts with its designated letter. What words that begin with that letter come to mind for you when contemplating God's light? Each line can be just one word, a phrase, or even a full sentence—totally up to you! And please remember, you cannot do this wrong. If you're prone to overthinking or a strong inner critic, consider moving quickly, spending no more than ten minutes writing the poem, as moving quickly will help you outpace your overthinking or inner critic.

Prompt 3

Close your eyes. Breathe deeply. Allow yourself a few moments of quiet and stillness, where all you hear, all you feel, is your steady inhale and exhale. Ask God to open your imagination to Him.

God's goodness is the light we need in our lives. To really wrap our hearts around the idea that God accepts all of who we are, I think we have to let His goodness seep into our bones. Consider verses like these:

- "I would have lost heart, unless I had believed that I would see the goodness of the LORD in the land of the living" (Ps. 27:13 NKJV).
- "Taste and see that the LORD is good; blessed is the one who takes refuge in him" (Ps. 34:8).
- "The LORD, the LORD God, merciful and gracious, longsuffering, and abounding in goodness and truth" (Ex. 34:6 NKJV).
- "Surely goodness and mercy shall follow me all the days of my life; and I will dwell in the house of the LORD forever" (Ps. 23:6 NKJV).

- “The Lord is good to all, and His tender mercies are over all His works” (Ps. 145:9 NKJV).
- “Every good gift and every perfect gift is from above, and comes down from the Father of lights, with whom there is no variation or shadow of turning” (James 1:17 NKJV).
- “For He satisfies the longing soul, and fills the hungry soul with goodness” (Ps. 107:9 NKJV).
- “For He knows our frame; He remembers that we are dust” (Ps. 103:14 NKJV).
- “Hear me, O Lord, for Your lovingkindness is good; turn to me according to the multitude of Your tender mercies” (Ps. 69:16 NKJV).

Sit in the goodness of those truths for as long as your heart needs. Then, begin to slow and deepen your breathing. Close your eyes and begin to really settle into this moment, into the space you’re in. Remind yourself there’s no rush or hurry here. The invitation is to simply sit in stillness and quiet. Imagine God’s goodness spreading like a warm, gentle light over you. As you sit with Him, in His presence, know that He welcomes all of you—your pain, your questions, your heart, your thoughts. You may just simply want to sit in His presence. Or, you may have a desire to talk with Him, to listen to His heart for you. Stay with Him for as long as you want, and when you’re ready, slowly open your eyes, and put pen to page to journal about this time.

CHAPTER 6

The Path to Healing:

Leaving Shame at the Well

Shame dies when stories are told in safe spaces.

~Ann Voskamp

Shame is a relentless weed that, left unattended, chokes out goodness. Brené Brown defines "shame as the intensely painful feeling or experience of believing that we are flawed and therefore unworthy of love and belonging—something we've experienced, done, or failed to do makes us unworthy of connection."[1]

As I began to taste healing at the edges of my story, as the fog of grief and depression began to dissipate, I saw the collateral damage, as if a hurricane had swept through the relationships I cherished most, scattering debris and brokenness around us.

Shame flushed over my cheeks, thinking of how little my children were and how little choice they'd had in being in this part of my story.

Too young to read it or understand it, but needing a starting point to process everything, I wrote my children a confession. This letter is a window into how I began sorting through my shame with Jesus.

My Dear Wildly Precious Children,

This is a confession to you, my kids, about what I know I'm not good at. It's an apology of sorts. It's an *I wish these weren't my struggles, so that they weren't a part of your story* confession. It's a *taking ownership of my own flaws* manifesto. I want you to know that I know. It's so important to me that you know I'm not making excuses. That I am painfully aware of the ways in which I fall short. I know, and it pains me, down to my core.

Even though I can't be perfect, I still wish I could be for you. Even though I know that perseverance produces character, and character hope, I wish in an aching way that I could will my weaknesses away. That I could perfectly balance the demands and stressors of every day in breathtaking grace and humility.

But too often, I walk around demanding that the world conform to me and responding as though you and the world owe me something when it all goes wrong. I walk around like my annoyances and irritations should be the rest of the world's grievances. I walk around as if I own the place, and everyone else should bend and flex to my preferences.

And in the mundane, ordinary of each day, it's so easy to trade relationships for orders, for telling you what to do, what not to do, and how to respond. But I'm desperate for you to know, that you are known and you are loved, by me, by your dad, and by your heavenly Father. I want you to know that you are safe, warm, recognized, loved, affirmed, and secure because you are God's first and ours second.

I know that life can't be perfect for anyone. But I've also known for a long time that my life has been skewed too far the other direction, like a plodding, sometimes angry, kicking donkey. I'm learning how to let limitations and boundaries landscape my life. How to be at soul-rest because I am deeply loved by God. How to stop and listen long enough to know what my soul is thirsty for. And now here, even in this space of still uncertainty, still searching, still yearning, still not fully knowing, I can see with the full-scale color of my imagination once again that tending to our souls is the greatest and most beautiful demand put on our lives.

Love,

Mama

What Shame Does to Our Brains and Why Journaling Can Help

Curt Thompson defines shame as "silent, subtle, and characterized by the quiet self-condemning conversation that we've learned since we were kids . . . impairing our ability to deal with other aspects of life in a healthy way. . . . [We] turn inward and away from other people, disintegrating [ourselves] from them."[2]

From a spiritual perspective, Thompson continues, "Evil's intention is not just to make us feel worse than we should—it's to devour the universe. It wants everything."[3] Left unchecked, evil will twist and distort our stories until we're utterly convinced that we are without hope or a way forward.

While I had a moment of clarity and healing with Jesus when I could visualize Him being present with me in my pain, I still had to work through the collateral damage that resulted from my years of unprocessed grief and trauma. I had to reclaim the ground that the enemy had tried to take.

Journaling became the practice through which God wrote new lines of grace into my story. Journaling is one experience that allows us to, as Deborah Ross explains, "harness the power of . . . pen or keyboard . . . to stimulate healing, vitality, resilience, and growth."[4] Left unrenewed, our minds will continue to wear in the same familiar ruts day after day, often trapping us in our pain, unresolved issues, and shame. But, as we'll explore more fully later in this chapter, journaling rewires our brains toward goodness, wholeness, and abundant life in Christ.

The Paradox of the Gospel

Shame tries to convince us that the whole story is written, there's nothing more to see or learn—just the same old weary, worn-out story. But in Christ, our stories are always teeming with possibility and redemption. There are always new lines of grace to be written. We are never too late, too wrong, or too far gone. Because "there is therefore now no condemnation to them which are in Christ Jesus, who walk not after the flesh, but after the Spirit" (Rom. 8:1 King James Version).

What a beautiful paradox that two things can be simultaneously true. We've gotten it wrong *and* God loves us. We have broken trust *and* God does not condemn us. We have messed up *and* He's still writing a better story. To move forward, out of our shame and to trace the lines of grace, we must be able to hold two truths simultaneously.

Francis Weller illustrates this tension:

> The work of the mature person is to carry grief in one hand and gratitude in the other and to be stretched large by them. How much sorrow can I hold? That's how much gratitude I can give. If I carry only grief, I'll bend toward cynicism and despair. If I have only gratitude, I'll become saccharine and won't develop much compassion for other people's suffering. Grief keeps the heart fluid and soft, which helps make compassion possible.[5]

Grief and gratitude. Pain and softness. Loss and gain. Shame and redemption. We move through our shame by the paradox of the gospel. The counterintuitive nature of Jesus' kingdom is the only hope for making sense of the detours, wrong turns, and dead ends that so many of us have white knuckled our way through. But Paul reminds us that "anyone who believes in him will never be put to shame" (Rom. 10:11).

In Christ, our stories are always teeming with possibility and redemption. We are never too late, too wrong, or too far gone.

John 4: A Woman's Encounter with Jesus

Jesus and the Samaritan woman in John 4 are a paradox. In their culture, gender and religious associations divided them. The paradox for this woman at the well was that to heal, she had to let go of her old identity and instead find it in the One who would bear the marks of the cross to free her forever.

Jesus, weary from travel, sits down at a well in Samaria. He is a Savior who can identify with our own human weariness. This woman comes to the well as part of her daily, necessary routine, but at a time when she assumes no one else will be there. Maybe she avoids the crowds because she cannot avoid the indignity of being an outcast. Her hope is perhaps fragile, far outpaced by her shame.

Jesus asks for a drink, and in her practicality, she rebuffs Him twice. She points out that He is a Jew and she, a Samaritan. When He is not ruffled by the social taboo, she tries the practical approach by pointing out that He has "nothing to draw water with" (John 4:11 ESV).

Jesus redirects her: "Everyone who drinks of this water will be thirsty again, but whoever drinks of the water that I will give him will never be thirsty again. The water that I will give him will become in him a spring of water welling up to eternal life" (vv. 13–14 ESV).

The woman's answer is telling: "Sir, give me this water, so that I will not be thirsty or have to come here to draw water" (v. 15 ESV). So focused on her material needs and the possibility of an easier life, she struggles to see who is right before her, right there with her.

When Jesus tells her to go get her husband, her honest response aches with the wounds of life: "I have no husband" (v. 17 ESV). She dwells on externals of identity, and He yearns for her to see His true identity. She dwells on the hardships and inconveniences of life. He yearns for her to be fully satisfied in Him. Jesus persists with this woman because He knows that He is her only hope for moving out of shame and into the fullness of life in Him.

As their encounter continues, Jesus says to her, "You are right when you say you have no husband, for you have had five husbands, and the one you now have is not your husband" (vv. 17–18 ESV). It's as if Jesus is saying to her, "'I'm willing to go with you where you're not even willing to go.'"[6] For what we might presume is much of her adult life, this woman has turned away from those in her community—or perhaps been turned away by them. In a vicious cycle fueled by shame, she had been embracing the lie that she is not worthy to be one of them.

She says to Jesus, "I perceive that you are a prophet" (v. 19). She recognizes that He's special but doesn't yet see that He is the Messiah. Then Jesus reveals to her that He is in fact the Messiah (v. 26).

Jesus pours living water out for this woman to quench the shame-filled lies. In His interaction with her, we witness Him do for her what He does for all of us, as Curt Thompson says, "Responding to our shame by drawing us out of it and into community with him first and then others."[7]

In John 4:27 their story continues: "Just then his disciples came back. They marvled that he was talking with a woman, but no one said, 'What do you seek?' or 'Why are you talking with her?'"

The disciples, who always have questions for Jesus, ask none here. I'm so in trigued. Could it be that they recognize the sacred moment transpiring between Jesus and this woman? For the first time in her life, she is drinking in true, living water and she is being transformed. She is exchanging the stagnant water of shame for the living water of Jesus Christ.

By letting the living water of Jesus run through her, the Samaritan woman traded her old identity for one securely held in Christ.

She leaves her jug and hurries back to town with this message: "Come, see a man who told me everything that I ever did. Can this be the Christ?" (vv. 28–29). Something so significant transpired in this woman's encounter with Jesus that she left her water jar behind. By letting the living water of Jesus run through her, she trades her old identity for one securely held in Christ.

John 4:39 provides our last glance into the Samaritan woman's new life: "Many Samaritans from that town believed in him because of the woman's testimony, 'He told me all that I ever did.'" First, this woman acknowledges the source of her shame in the healing presence of Jesus. Then, she moves out into her community to tell them who had healed her shame. An entire community is changed through this healing encounter. As Curt Thompson articulates, "We need others in order for our shame to be healed and for us to have the chance to move past it."[8]

We, like this woman, slump under the weight of the identities we weren't created to bear. We have past mistakes and regrets that swamp our souls with shame. We'd prefer a quick fix or an escape route to an easier life, a lighter load, a more glamorous identity. We fail to realize it's not *what* we need but *who* we need. What Jesus says about us is truer than any diagnosis, label, or mistake can attest to. He says that we are wholly His, free of our shame, and set free to have abundant life in Him.

In the quiet of our hearts, shame creeps up our necks and turns inward on our hearts. Shame hisses the lie that we are only the sum of all our bad decisions, those choices that have us tangled up, that brought chaos and emptiness instead of fulfillment. Curt Thompson reminds us:

> The problem is when I find myself alone with the thoughts in my head . . . I can still feel deep shame that goes beyond healthy remorse. This is why the Crucifixion and Jesus' naked body is such a big deal. Even in our artwork depicting the event, we don't strip him naked. We have a loincloth around him, and that's all well and good, but it suggests that we don't want God going that far. But he does. God himself submitted to the shame of the Cross. He has been there. And he says, "I'm willing to go with you where you're not even willing to go."[9]

As I journaled through Reed's diagnosis and its aftermath, I could see that journaling was helping me to heal from the inside out. Plenty of research—like sociologist and professor Dr. James Pennebaker's book *Writing to Heal*—has shown us that writing does help us heal. But by the time I turned thirty-seven, about a decade after Reed's diagnosis, I became intent on understanding *why* writing could heal. I'd experienced it firsthand, and now I wanted to understand what was transpiring between my pen, my mind, and God. I sought to understand how simply putting my thoughts down on paper could metabolize my pain and, in turn, God could make it into something beautiful.

The answer is found in the word *neuroplasticity*. Therapists Ross and Adams define "neuroplasticity [as] the ability of the brain to change its structure in response to experience."[10] Have you ever felt like you are stuck in a rut? There's a good reason—as I mentioned earlier, our brains actually do form ruts, so to speak. Our neural pathways are what allow the different areas of our brains to connect and communicate.

Well-worn neural pathways fire quickly and efficiently. So, for example, you don't have to think very hard about brushing your teeth because that is a well-formed connection in your brain from years of standing in front of the bathroom mirror with toothbrush in hand. This efficiency is less helpful if the patterns or habits negatively impact our mental well-being. If stress habitually leads you into micromanaging, drill sergeant mode, that brain connection is reinforced with each trip down that path.

But neuroplasticity means we can strengthen the neural pathways that bring us goodness and wholeness by rerouting our patterns of thinking and acting. This is good news because it means we are not stuck in our brokenness or despair. I think this is exactly what Romans 12:2 means when it says we should "be transformed by the renewing of your mind." To change the ruts we find ourselves in we must intentionally make new connections in our brains through wisdom, insight, and experience, which is exactly what journaling offers us.

Until I began studying journaling with the Therapeutic Writing Institute, I primarily journaled through free writing. Whatever was on my mind, I transcribed that onto paper. Whenever I felt the urge to write. Whenever I had a prayer that begged to be released on paper. Whenever I was so overcome with emotion that nothing but writing would help, I would journal. No prompt. No structure. Just get all my thoughts out on paper.

Sometimes that seemed helpful; other times, I felt discouraged and disappointed because I kept looping through the same ideas. While open-ended journaling is commonplace, if you're facing deep emotional pain or trauma or even just feel stuck in your journaling practice, this free-writing style may be unhelpful. When you feel overwhelmed, structured journaling with a clear framework is often better suited to help you move through your pain and find peace. Journaling with gentle guidance provides safety, boundaries, and direction.

Imagine the scaffolding used as buildings are being erected. It provides a way for the incomplete building to be worked on. The scaffolding allows the engineers and construction crews to safely reach places they couldn't otherwise. Likewise, structured journaling can be your scaffolding to explore with God the contours of your story and heart, especially the hard places.

Like a pace car in a race that sets the speed at which the racers can go in a safety lap, structured journaling allows you to slowly and intentionally explore difficult emotions. Structured journaling creates emotionally safe experiences that signal to the brain it's okay to name, write down, and explore hard things. When we practice more structured, guided journaling, we can slowly and steadily build up the fortitude and muscles needed for deeper, longer, more open-ended journaling.

Journaling through metaphor, like we've been exploring in this book, is a structured framework of putting our thoughts on the page. If you've felt stuck in your journaling or like journaling hasn't served you as well as you'd hope, journaling through metaphor may be the key that unlocks your mind and heart to experience the presence of God in ways that redeem and transform your life.

JOURNALING PROMPTS

Prompt 1

Write a letter of confession. This letter can be addressed to yourself, to God, or to another person. But I want you to write in at least one new or different way than you typically might. For example, if you always write in black ink, choose blue. Instead of writing from left to right or from top to bottom on a page, write in the opposite direction. If you always sit at your kitchen table to journal, pick a new spot. You may be curious why I'm asking you to do this. Sometimes, shifting our habitual practices is just enough novelty to open up new neural pathways in our brains, to spark new perspectives or ideas about stories we've rehearsed in our minds over and over.

Prompt 2

Using Jesus' living water metaphor from John 4, complete this prompt: Pouring Living Water over my shame is like . . .

Prompt 3

Close your eyes. Breathe deeply. Allow yourself a few moments of quiet and stillness, where all you hear, all you feel, is your steady inhale and exhale. Ask God to open your imagination to Him.

Find moving water. Have you ever eased yourself into a warm bath and felt your body relax? Or, stood mesmerized by the seemingly infinite ocean? Or felt more at peace sitting by a steam? Our own experiences and science confirm that water can lower our stress goes down and enliven our minds.[11] This could be your kitchen faucet. This could be a river, stream, creek, or waterfall. Even a video of moving water will work. In that space, take a moment to look around and if you're willing, dip your hands, your feet, or maybe even your whole body into the water. Inhale and exhale deeply. Close your eyes, and let the tension you're holding release as you breathe deeply. Imagine that Jesus is with you. What comes to mind for you in this space? Is it peace and gratitude? Welcome it. Is it worries or regrets? Acknowledge them. Remind yourself that you are safe and known because Jesus is with you. Ask Jesus to show you your belovedness, redemption, and wholeness in Him. Ask Him simply to meet you in this ordinary space, to help you know in your bones that He sees you, He knows you, He loves you. That He is Living Water that will replenish your weary soul. Stay in this space with Him as long as you want, and when you're ready, open your eyes and begin writing, pouring your heart out to Him.

CHAPTER 7

The Practice of Journaling:

Come to the Table

Taken, blessed, broken, given "is the shape of the communion table. This is the shape of the Gospel. This is the shape of the Christian life."

~Eugene Peterson

"Do you journal regularly?" I asked the woman sitting across from me. A group of ten of us had gathered at a local coffee shop for a night of journaling and coffee.

"Not as much as I should," she responded. And then, after a thoughtful pause,

"But I want to. And that's why I'm here tonight." Some version of this is what I hear from so many people when we discuss journaling. They have the desire but not the time. Or they have the desire but not the consistency. They recognize the value of journaling but have yet to ingrain it as a normal habit or rhythm in their lives.

Through six chapters, you've been learning about the power and ubiquity of metaphor, journaling, and experiencing God's presence through Scripture's metaphors. If you've journaled through the prompts at the end of each chapter, you've been engaged with this deeply transformative practice. I hope, at this point, you're beginning to see the beauty and benefit of putting pen to page in this unique way. I hope you're beginning to imagine how this practice, if done regularly, can enrich your soul and life. How it can connect you to God's healing presence.

I want to offer practical suggestions for creating and cultivating this practice long after you turn the last page of this book.

A Four-Step Framework

James Clear, the New York Times bestselling author of *Atomic Habits*, says that "Rewards are the end goal of every habit."[1] According to Clear, there's a repeatable process anyone can use to turn a wishful desire into a practice of life that nourishes you:

1. *Cue:* make it obvious
2. *Craving:* make it attractive
3. *Response:* make it easy
4. *Reward:* make it satisfying

Cue: Make It Obvious

Since we moved into our home seven years ago, it has been in a constant state of renovation. My husband has almost single-handedly taken our 1966-built ranch home into the twenty-first century by knocking down walls, laying new flooring, insulating, drywalling, rearranging, painting, installing new windows, all to rebuild it to be both functional and beautiful.

Most recently, he's transformed what was a very small bedroom on our first floor into walk-in closets and expanded bathroom space. During the renovation, I had to relocate my clothes to temporary storage. After the renovation, as I unpacked my clothes I discovered one of my favorite sweaters that had been stored away. This sweater is super soft and lightweight, and the most beautiful shade of deep pink—the perfect sweater for a slightly cool fall day. I really, really love this sweater.

But it had been out of my sight for over a month. When something is out of my sight, it is also most definitely out of mind. When I rediscovered that sweater, I was elated, almost as much as when I first bought the sweater and started wearing it. Do you know where that sweater stays now? In the front of my closet, in an obvious spot where I see it regularly, so that I can easily remember to wear it.

Much like my beloved sweater, if I'm going to journal, I need to leave my journal out in plain sight, to keep it an obvious spot where I will be easily cued to pick it up and write in it. For me, that means putting my journal either on my kitchen table if I'm going to be home or in my leather tote bag if I'm going to be out and about. You just never know when the opportunity to journal might pop up. It's easiest for me to write in the small in-between spaces of my day—while I drink my

While journaling should not have the same level of priority as Scripture, even the Bible underscores the importance of making the things we value obvious.

morning coffee, the few minutes I have between teaching classes, or as I wait in the car line to pick my children up. Or, at my kitchen table so that long after dinner dishes have been cleared, dogs have been fed, and kids have been put to bed, I can steal five or ten minutes to write.

"Tie [God's commandments] as symbols on your hands and bind them on your foreheads. Write them on the door-frames of your houses and on your gates" (Deut. 6:8–9). While journaling should not have the same level of priority as Scripture, even the Bible underscores the importance of making the things we value obvious.

Where can you place your journal so that it will be obvious?

Craving: Make It Attractive

Beauty. We are wired for it. Drawn to it. Attracted by it. We crave it. According to a study noted by *BBC Science Focus*, "When the participants experienced beautiful images or music, the researchers saw activity in a region of the brain called the medial orbitofrontal cortex, which plays a role in our feelings of reward and pleasure."[2]

Why are HGTV home renovation shows so wildly popular? Because they show us beautifully done spaces. Why do we seek out crystal blue waters and soft, white sand for vacations? Because we love beautiful places. Why do we post pictures of beautiful meals on Instagram? Because we eat with our eyes first. David underscores this reality in Psalm 27:4: "One thing I ask from the Lord, this only do I seek: that I may dwell in the house of the LORD all the days of my life, to gaze on the beauty of the LORD and to seek him in his temple."

How can we apply this to building the habit of journaling? Buy beautiful journals. This does not mean they have to be expensive. Some of my most beloved journals have been purchased at CVS. Do you love flowers and dappled things? Or do you prefer the simple beauty of a monochromatic cover? Do you like smooth, glossy covers or rippled texture that you can run your fingers over? Maybe you want a fat, thick, lined journal that will last you for at least a year. Or perhaps you prefer small, slim, unlined journals. The point is, you get to figure out what is beautiful to you when it comes to what you write in. Research suggests that if it catches your eye, you are more likely to pick it up and use it.

Where you journal can also be a source of beauty. Maybe that's simply sitting on your back porch listening to birds and seeing beautiful trees and plants and flowers. Or maybe it's creating a reading and journaling nook in your home, with your favorite mug, a cozy blanket, and a stack of books. Maybe it's your favorite coffee shop with gorgeous art on the walls. While all humans are drawn to beauty, we all find beauty in different ways. What do you find beautiful, and where do you find beauty? Journaling with beauty will make the work of establishing this practice easier for you.

Response: Make Your Yes Easy

When my friend Chloe asked if I'd be willing to lead a few journaling sessions at her women's ministry retreat at a beach house in Gulf Shores, Alabama, that was an easy yes. Why? Well, first, Chloe's a dear friend. Second, we were going to a

If knowing your why is the 10,000-foot view of forming a new habit, then having a plan is the ground-level, get-moving step.

beautiful beach house, and if I can be anywhere, the beach is always my first choice. Third, leading journaling sessions is one of my absolute favorite things to do. A dear friend, time at the beach, and journaling? Check, check, check. That yes response to Chloe was incredibly easy.

How can you make your yes to journaling exponentially easier?

Good coaching usually starts with this maxim: Know your why. Michael Hyatt reminds us that "motivation is the key to forming any habit. If we get lost in the monotony and difficulty of forming a habit, we're not going to make it. The messy middle swamps countless goal seekers. . . . A compelling *why* will prevent us from burning out or losing interest and quitting. If your *why* is not compelling enough, it's time to swap it for something that excites you."[3] Building your journaling practice will be easier if you can articulate your why.

Why do you want to journal? There's no right or wrong answer to this question, and your answer can be simple (I love beautiful journals) or more complex (I need an outlet for my creativity). You may discover you have multiple reasons why or even that your reasons ebb and flow over time. What's important is that you do find *your* compelling reason because it makes it that much easier to say yes to something you value.

If knowing your *why* is the 10,000-foot view of forming a new habit, then having a plan is the ground-level, get-moving step. Several years ago, I wanted to reboot my reading of Scripture, which had grown lax and spotty. I love Scripture, but amid family life and work demands, sustaining that habit can be challenging for me.

Several friends recommended one particular plan, and I gamely—if somewhat skeptically—began the challenge of reading through the Bible in a year. But, opening my Bible each day and knowing exactly which passages to read for the plan was so freeing and helpful, making it far easier to say yes to that discipline. Also? Because the plan was available in the Bible app, I could easily listen to the day's Scripture reading. The plan made my yes easy.

Could the same be true for your journaling? What plan will make your yes to journaling an easy one?

The Power of Community

In the pandemic lockdown of 2020, with no option to physically go to the gym, my sister and cousin began video calling each other every morning to exercise together. They'd each cue up the same exercise video and through FaceTime work out together. Simply put, they were creating community around a habit they wanted to keep.

Most people recognize the value of community. It's why AA has weekly meetings for its members to attend. Why many churches emphasize the importance of community or small groups. Why social media makes it easier and easier to connect with people who live in your community or who share your interest in hiking or knitting. People want to be together, sharing common interests, doing the things they love or want to love, and dissolving old habits and replacing them with better ones.

Maybe you think of journaling as a solitary—rather than communal—activity, and in one sense, I agree with you. A sense of privacy is essential for effective journaling because only when we sense that our words are safe are we willing to be honest. And being honest is crucial for journaling that will help us see clearly and heal. As my journaling mentor Kathleen Adams is fond of saying, journaling should help us tell "the complete truth faster."[4] Journaling that falls short of the complete truth is counterfeit. However, not journaling at all, because you can't seem to get the habit to stick, lands you far shorter of the goal than anything else.

One of the first questions my health coach asked me when we started working together was, "How do the people around you eat?" We both knew if what's being served up around me is fried foods and sweet treats, that's probably what I'm going to eat. But if I'm surrounded by other people who are eating grilled fish and fresh fruit, I'm more likely to make that choice. When we're with others who value what we value and we are in turn given an opportunity to do the same thing, we're more likely to establish it as a habit we can enjoy for years to come.

I meet weekly online with a small group of people to journal. Once a month, I meet in person with people in a local coffee shop to journal together. A couple of times a year, I host journaling retreats so that people can get away, be together, and journal.

But if we're just writing side by side, is that effective? A concept known as body doubling supports the effectiveness of all three of these journaling gatherings. While body doubling is usually suggested as a motivator for those with ADHD, I've seen it benefit a variety of people, neurodivergent or not. According to PsychCentral, body doubling "is having another person around while you work on a task. They don't have to assist directly; just simply being present could help you start, focus, and finish."[5]

I can personally attest to the effectiveness of this strategy. You're holding this book in your hands, in large part, because of a simple Thursday morning routine I've held for over two years now. Most Thursdays, my dear friend Deborah and I meet online, chat for a few minutes about what's happening in our lives, and then spend the next couple of hours writing silently together. The consistency and accountability of that Thursday morning session are, quite literally, how this book got written.

Reward: Make It Satisfying

What makes journaling satisfying for me? It's finding a place for the misplaced, mismatched thoughts I'm ruminating on. Building a refuge for my tenderest emotions. Stitching grace over weariness. It's seeing in plain sight how God is working in my life. But I also find satisfaction in finding just the right type of journal to write in. The pages must be lined. The paper must be thick enough that ink won't bleed through, but also soft enough that my pen glides smoothly across it.

Recently, I've changed the kind of journal I write in. Previously, I bought a giant, hardbound journal that I would use to journal in throughout the entire calendar year. Even though I loved the idea of having one whole year of my thoughts bound in one book, practically, that size journal was cumbersome to tote around (and I do take my journal almost everywhere I go). Plus, trying to locate a specific journal entry later could be time-consuming. So, now I buy a sixteen-pack bundle of small, 8x5-inch soft-cover journals that each contain ninety-two pages, and I use one of those for each month of the year to journal. I find it satisfying to close one journal at the end of each month and begin a fresh one the next month. Also, I love to see the small stack of green, soft-cover journals grow month by month on my bookshelf.

Our habitual practices are the ones that keep us.

Just like each person has a different take on beauty, each of us may differ on what makes a practice of journaling satisfying. If you're not sure, spend some time thinking about that. Or, look at it in reverse, and consider what has made journaling feel unsatisfying before. Remember, your answer to this might be simple (*I like the feel of the pen moving across the page*) or more complex (*I like to see my thoughts on paper so I can better sort them out*) or maybe a combination of a few different reasons.

What will make the practice of journaling satisfying for you? Seasons of life ebb and flow. Good seasons, hard seasons, and often both, intermingle. Our habitual practices are the ones that keep us. This practice of experiencing the presence of God through journaling Scripture's metaphors can be one of those rhythms, as Ann Voskamp suggests, that "keep your soul from growing threadbare . . . [to] fight through the waves of life."[6]

Why Making This a Habit Matters

Recently, I was asked where I feel most like myself. Immediately, I thought of my mom's kitchen table. Most Sundays growing up, my mom would slow-cook a pot roast and simmer a pot of green beans until they had the sweetest and best flavor you can imagine, served up with a side of rice and a pitcher of sweet tea. I was fascinated by adult conversation around that table, and as I grew into a high schooler and then college student, I'd gather with a gaggle of friends around my mom's table to eat my other favorite dish (her spaghetti), play cards, and stay up until the wee hours of the night talking, laughing, and dreaming.

In those early years after Reed's diagnosis, when we still lived in Pennsylvania, there was nothing I missed or looked forward to more than sitting around my mom's kitchen table when we'd come home for a visit. So many of life's waves were processed through and comforted by the food, conversations, and prayers shared around her table.

In my own kitchen, underneath the clutter of family life, is a table my husband built out of American Wormy Chestnut. That table is beautiful and holds significance for our family. Not only does it give us a functional place to eat our meals, but it's also the primary gathering place for our family. School projects. Game nights. Early morning and late-night conversations. Journaling.

Our times at kitchen tables are not just romanticized nostalgia, especially those made from natural materials. Scientists have found that "wood reduced blood pressure and heart rate. The body, sensing something organic, slows down. Wood has visual depth—grain, knots, texture—which invites what scientists call 'soft fascination.' It's the opposite of doomscrolling. It's watching light move across oak. It's your fingers tracing a dent in an old table."[7]

Both the once living tree-turned-table and the lived lives of those who gather around it are significant, a reminder that our tables can be sacred spaces for life.

The most significant event in the life of Jesus was His death and resurrection. And, as N. T. Wright wrote, "When Jesus himself wanted to explain to his disciples what his forthcoming death was all about, he didn't give them a theory, he gave them a meal."[8] He invited them to the table, into His presence:

> While they were eating, Jesus took bread, and when he had given thanks, he broke it and gave it to his disciples, saying, "Take and eat; this is my body."

> Then he took a cup, and when he had given thanks, he gave it to them, saying, "Drink from it, all of you. This is my blood of the covenant, which is poured out for many for the forgiveness of sins. I tell you, I will not drink from this fruit of the vine from now on until that day when I drink it new with you in my Father's kingdom." (Matt. 26:26–29)

Jesus took the most ordinary, concrete items—bread and wine—to bring the reality of the kingdom of God right to the disciples' dinner table. Prior to this dinner, Jesus referred to Himself as the living bread (John 6:51), as the food that never perishes, that ultimately satisfies and brings about true life for those who will eat it.

In John 6:35, Jesus declared, "I am the bread of life. Whoever comes to me will never go hungry, and whoever believes in me will never be thirsty." In this, I see God's provision. Jesus is our manna. He nourishes our very beings. In our never-enough, Jesus invites us into His abundant, more-than-enough, His bread-of-life enough.

But those listening to Jesus found His words hard to swallow, as if they were choking on stale breadcrumbs instead of consuming the life-giving bread of Christ. "On hearing [he was the Bread of Life], many of His disciples said, 'This is a hard teaching. Who can accept it?'" (John 6:60). But Jesus' earlier words remain: "I am the living bread that came down from heaven" (John 6:51).

After the crowds and the Jews in the synagogues turned away from Him, Jesus turned to His disciples: "You do not want to leave too, do you?" (John 6:67). Jesus pointed straight to their hearts, just as He points to ours. We can choose to stay connected to Jesus, who will sustain us in our present circumstances, or we can choose our own way, disconnected from Him as the source of life.

To Jesus' question, Peter responded, "Lord, to whom shall we go? You have the words of eternal life" (John 6:68). Let's affirm with Peter that coming to Christ's table, we can find peace and courage within our souls. So, we come to His table. With all of our questions and uncertainties. With all of our fears and anxieties. With all of our weaknesses and failures and questions, we can say, Jesus, I "have learned to believe and trust . . . that You are the Holy One of God, the Christ (the Anointed One), the Son of the living God" (John 6:69 AMPC). Because Jesus is both the provider and the provision, let's come meet Him at His table of blessing.[9]

JOURNAL PROMPTS

Prompt 1

Use James Clear's framework to help you consistently come to the journaling table:

- Cue: How will I remind myself to journal?
- Craving: How can I incorporate beauty into my journaling rhythm?
- Response: What plan will I use for journaling?
- Reward: What, for me, is the reward of journaling?

Prompt 2

Can you think for a moment about the tables you've sat at throughout your life? The one in your childhood home. The one in the school cafeteria. The one at church potluck dinners. The one in your first home as a young adult. The first one you and your spouse picked out together. The one that your babies all teethed at. Let these tables meander through your mind. What were these tables like? What did you love about each one? What made some of them quirkier than others? What happened around these tables? What conversations were had? As you ponder these tables, pick one that you'd like to write about.

- Why did you pick this particular table?
- What did it look like?
- Who sat around it?
- What is most memorable to you about this table?
- What did you learn from sitting at this table?

Prompt 3

Close your eyes. Breathe deeply. Allow yourself a few moments of quiet and stillness, where all you hear, all you feel, is your steady inhale and exhale. Ask God to open your imagination to Him.

As Jesus invited His disciples to come to the table of "blessing, breaking, and giving,"[10] so, too, are we. Close your eyes and begin to breathe deeply, filling your lungs through your nose and then slowly releasing your breath through your mouth. Breathe in this pattern two or three more times, allowing your body and mind and heart to release any tension it may be holding. In this quiet space you've settled into, imagine that this is a table that Jesus has set for you—a table of blessing, breaking, and giving. A table for you to bring your whole self to—all of blessed, broken, given you. He has set this table as the Bread of Life to nourish you.

How do you feel coming to and sitting at this table with the Bread of Life? What does this table He's set look like? Can you listen intently for what conversation He wants to have with you?

Remember, those who come to Him will never be hungry or thirsty. He is your manna. When you come to His table, you stay connected to Jesus, the source of your life. For all your questions, your worries, your needs—for all of you—He has the words of eternal life, of peace and courage.

You are invited to stay in this moment, in this space, experiencing all His table and His words have to offer, for as long as you like. There is no hurry, nor any rush to leave the table set before you.

When you're ready, you can open your eyes and begin writing about your experience of coming to the table.[11]

CHAPTER 8

Pushing Through Obstacles:

Keeping Pen to Page

Habits are the invisible architecture of everyday life.

~Gretchen Rubin

At some point, you will discover that days, weeks, or months have passed since you cracked open your journal. But journaling will bend and flex with your seasons of life. Only have five minutes to jot off some quick thoughts? Your journal is willing and ready. God, who can multiply a meager serving of fish and bread, enough to feed 5,000, can surely multiply your five minutes into something worthwhile and meaningful.

What keeps you—or has kept you—from journaling? Perhaps you have the desire and good intentions, but you keep falling out of the rhythm. Or maybe even knowing its benefits and enjoying it, you just can't seem to find your way back to the page. You might keep telling yourself that you're going to get back to it, and yet, that time never seems to come. You keep buying the next new guided journal, stick with it for two or three days (maybe a couple of weeks if you're really determined), and then it joins the rest of the barely started, certainly never finished, journals that sit on your bookshelf. Ask me how I know. Or better yet, ask my husband about how many stacks upon stacks of half-finished journals I have on our bookshelf.

Can You Name the Obstacle?

One good question to ask is: *What is actually keeping me from journaling?* How many reasons do you think you could come up with? Five, ten, fifteen? What about 100?

You heard me right! Could you make a list of 100 obstacles that keep you from journaling? Kay Adams, in her book *Journal to the Self,* teaches this practice for the insights you'll gain. An audacious number like 100 invites your mind to dig a little deeper, and you'll probably be surprised at what you can mine from this kind of exploration. Gaining a clear sense of what exactly is standing in your way of really journaling like you want to will help you begin to build a bridge from where you are (not journaling) to where you want to be (in a regular rhythm of journaling). And, this is really important: It's okay to repeat items on the list. Repetition is an intrinsic part of the process for writing a list of 100; let yourself repeat (repeatedly). You'll have the chance to make this list as part of the prompts at the end of this chapter.

Why Is It You Want to Journal, Anyway?

While taking inventory of your situation is worthwhile and a necessary first step, another important question is: *Why do I want to journal?* Ask any habit guru or self-help coach what it takes to stick with a habit, and they'll likely tell you to home in on your why.

Why do you want to journal? Is it because your therapist has told you to? Is it because you think it's what you're supposed to do? Is it something that's worked in the past and you want it to work again? These can all be legitimate reasons. But I think we might need to dig a little deeper and get to the heart of the matter. Get to *your* heart on the matter.

At the end of this chapter, you'll have the opportunity to journal about your why. Whatever reason you pinpoint, knowing your why is the first step to pushing against the obstacles that are keeping you from writing.

But for now, I want to suggest one of the best reasons to journal might be staring back at you from the page. Why journal? Because through journaling's invitation to slow down, we find the stillness and attention we need to be with God in His presence.

Through journaling's invitation to slow down, we find the stillness and attention we need to be with God in His presence.

You've been learning through this book that journaling is a path into the presence of God. In His presence we find rest. In His presence is fullness of joy. In His presence, we are fully accepted, known, and loved. In His presence, we can begin to make sense of our stories. In His presence, we can find healing.

As I write this book, I'm fresh from a weekend journaling retreat where these very things happened. Not just for me, but for the other eleven women who stepped away from their full lives and for three days rested, shared meals, wrote in their journals, and gave witness to each other's stories. While it never takes much to convince me to take a weekend at the beach, many of these women had to overcome significant obstacles to be there. Anxiety. Hurricanes (there were two within the four weeks leading up to the retreat). Conflicting emotions about God. Overfull schedules. Coming alone. Tiredness. Sickness. Doubt. Confusion. Uncertainty about what even happens at a journaling retreat. Family concerns sitting in the corners of their minds, tugging at their hearts.

And yet, God in His kindness brought the twelve of us together. He gently led each one of us through our obstacles to the weekend together He had prepared for us. In the unhurried pace of His grace, we slowed down, savored stillness, and listened for the whisper of the Holy Spirit. We put our pens to the page to trace the thread of grace being woven through our stories. We cried salty tears. We made honest, raw confessions. We hugged each other and made a toast to journaling. We witnessed anger dissolving. Grief being tended. The delight of fresh insight emerging.

We drove to the Airbnb, laid down our bags and our obligations, pulled out our journals, and asked God to meet us there. None knew where their pen would lead them. But we all were expecting that God would meet us, in the middle of our stories, on the middle of the page, and write grace into each line.

The Obstacles

Our best intentions get waylaid, *even when we have the best reason to make journaling happen.* Life is rife with obstacles. And our culture demands hustle and productivity, often at the expense of our physical, mental, and spiritual health. Even the apostle Paul recognizes our dilemma: "I do not understand what I do. For what I want to do I do not do, but what I hate I do" (Rom. 7:15). Let's see if we can unearth it a bit together.

Scenario 1

You decide you're going to rise every morning at 5 a.m. to read, pray, and journal. First morning, your eyes pop awake at 4:58 a.m., before your alarm even goes off. You slip out of bed, pick up your stack of books, nestle a warm mug of coffee, and settle into your favorite cozy spot. This feels good and right.

Second morning, your alarm has to wake you, but you still manage to slip out of bed and repeat yesterday's success. Morning three, you do it again. But by morning four, you're tapping snooze one, three, a dozen times. You still have enough time to get in twenty minutes of reading, praying, and journaling, which, you reason, is better than nothing.

Morning five, your youngest child pushes against your arm, while you're still sleepily tucked under your blanket. Rather than get up, you pull the child into bed with you, where you both promptly fall back asleep. Two weeks later, you've reverted to setting the alarm for 6 a.m., at which point your feet touch the ground, and you barely have a chance to pour your coffee, much less manage reading, praying, or journaling.

Sound familiar? I bet it does for so many of us. How do you typically respond to yourself and your inconsistencies? On hard days, I find myself frustrated and hopeless that I'll ever make it work. If that's you, too, I want to offer you a new line: *grace*, *compassion*, *curiosity*, and *reframe*. Instead of berating ourselves for our shortcomings, what if we met ourselves with these lines of grace?

- *Grace:* Life has a lot of demands.
- *Compassion:* New habits are hard to start. Trial and error, as well as experimentation, are a normal part of the process.
- *Curiosity:* What entices you to ignore the alarm? Gently exploring your answer can help you pinpoint the issue and perhaps even see a simple solution.
- *Reframe:* What other time of day may work better for you to journal?

Scenario 2

Someone suggested you try morning pages. Immediately upon waking, you take yourself to your desk, you pull out your pen and journal to begin writing. Your goal, as you've been told, is to fill three pages, stream-of-consciousness style. But, two lines in, you're stumped. Forget three pages! Or, your mind is brimming with ideas right up until you sit down to write. And then the thoughts evaporate along with any hope of getting those ideas down onto paper. Or, where do you even start? How do you even begin to unravel all these thoughts floating in your mind?

What if we met ourselves with these lines of grace?

- *Grace:* Getting started is usually the hardest step for most people, so you are not alone.
- *Compassion:* It's okay to feel like getting your thoughts down on paper is hard.
- *Curiosity:* Why is a blank page uninviting?
- *Reframe:* Not every method of journaling will work for every person in every season of life. When I teach journaling classes and workshops, I give everyone the permission not to like, love, or enjoy every journaling approach we try. I do encourage people to experiment and keep an open mind.

The Obstacle of Grief

Journaling has taught me that life is not a crisis to white-knuckle my way through but is a gift to be lived in God's good grip. As long as I viewed life as a crisis, my circumstances would merely be obstacles to the *good life* I wanted.

And yet, how do you walk this road faithfully when the grief is a long, living grief? When you wake up to the kind of new that rewrites, redefines, repurposes your life. A grief you don't outgrow.

This grief is sometimes imperceptible for days or months on end. Then one day, grief will peek out of her room and invite herself to breakfast.

Each time, her questions slide across the table like a plea bargain: *Are you going to be okay with God if your circumstances don't change? Will you be okay if God never explains why your story has these contours?*

Journaling has taught me that life is not a crisis to white-knuckle my way through but is a gift to be lived in God's good grip.

Yet, our grief is inextricably woven through with God's grace. His presence reshapes our grief. In the mystery of a God who loves us through deeply hard stories, grace refracts through pain like light through stained glass windows.

My expectations have given way to both the immense joy and the deafening heartache of loving someone with a rare genetic disorder. So, we trace the thread of God's grace through an often painful, sometimes impossible story of laying down our dreams of "normal" and "typical." We allow ourselves to feel the weight of our difficulties, but we also make space for the beauty and joy that comes in unexpected ways.

When grief sits across from me with her bagel and coffee, I remember that God's grace has always been sufficient. Even when the questions of why and how and how long are tightly tucked into my heart.

I pour grief another cup, and as I stir slowly, I press in: God is good, and God is present, and these two truths evidence a faithful God. His faithfulness is our provision through the obstacles.[1]

The Parable of the Sower

Scripture is not silent on the issue of obstacles. Consider the parable of the sower. This extended metaphor shows us that life in the kingdom can be hindered by obstacles. The people lining the shore to hear Jesus speak are invited "to consider the condition of their own hearts," as the Chara Project explains it.[2]

Jesus shares:

> "A farmer went out to sow his seed. As he was scattering the seed, some fell along the path; it was trampled on, and the birds ate it up.

> Some fell on rocky ground, and when it came up, the plants withered because they had no moisture. Other seed fell among thorns, which grew up with it and choked the plants. Still other seed fell on good soil. It came up and yielded a crop, a hundred times more than was sown." (Luke 8:5–8)

Jesus—the One who created language, who is the Word Himself—employs the power of metaphor to provoke potent understanding from everyday, lived experiences. Knowing His audience, He uses an agricultural picture to describe various spiritual conditions that are obstacles to the fullest expression of life in the kingdom. In Jesus' parable, the seed is vulnerable to three different obstacles: *what is stolen*, *what is cut short*, *what is overtaken.*

Do you believe you have been robbed of a good thing? This path is easy for any of us to walk down. We believe we are owed a good life, and when that dissipates, we often blame God. We turn away.

I've watched two friends in their early forties pass away this year, far too young, and leaving young families behind. Their lives, it seemed, cut short. It's tempting to turn away from God when death confuses and confounds us.

When we feel like our lives are burning, being overtaken by one fire after another, it's easy to want to simply give up. To let the raging flames have their way. To become numb and indifferent to the One whose heart is really on fire for us.

Jesus explains His metaphor:

> "This is the meaning of the parable: The seed is the word of God. Those along the path are the ones who hear, and then the devil comes and takes away the word from their hearts, so that they may not believe and be saved. Those on the rocky ground are the ones who receive

the word with joy when they hear it, but they have no root. They believe for a while, but in the time of testing they fall away. The seed that fell among thorns stands for those who hear, but as they go on their way they are choked by life's worries, riches and pleasures, and they do not mature. But the seed on good soil stands for those with a noble and good heart, who hear the word, retain it, and by persevering produce a crop." (Luke 8:11–15)

Jesus' parable acknowledges the brokenness of the world we live in. The reality and work of evil among us. The reality of difficulties and isolation. The reality of self-consumed desires. Jesus, with articulate precision, exposes these obstacles and their consequences to our lives in the kingdom. But this is not a parable that ends in death, at least not for the ones who open their lives and their hearts to the Word Himself. What Jesus offers at the end of this parable is a stunning gift of so much value that we can push past any obstacle to fully embrace Him.

> When we truly understand the abundant, soul-filling, life-giving gift God is offering us, we will push past our obstacles to be fully alive within the kingdom of God.

Jesus is helping people see that the kingdom of God, when it takes root in someone's heart, changes them. Changes what is possible in their lives. Really changes the result, the outcome, the very fruit of their lives. The Chara Project writers point out, "In this parable, the harvest most blatantly displays the heart of the sower. The abundant harvest multiplies as our hearts receive Christ, as His desires become our desires, and as we transform into sowers sharing the Kingdom of God with others!"[3] While the obstacles represented in this parable may seem overwhelming or disheartening, I love that really what Jesus wants most is for us to see the heart of God *for* us and what is possible *in* us when we abide with Him.

We are invited to look at our own hearts, the obstacles we may face, and then choose to cultivate a life where we can flourish in the kingdom of God. Dallas Willard exhorts us to "learn what it is within [us] that keeps [us] from being able to" be Christlike. "Perhaps it is that I have not devoted myself sufficiently to being alone with God, or to the taking in of his Word, so that I can actually trust Him to bless me when others are cursing me."[4]

When we truly understand the abundant, soul-filling, life-giving gift God is offering us, we will push past our obstacles to be fully alive within the kingdom of God.

What if journaling could be a practice that helps us push back against what is stolen, what is cut short, and what is overtaken? If, as I contend, journaling really is this life-giving practice that ushers us into the presence of God and brings vibrancy to our faith, then it is a practice worth fighting for. Worth pushing through the obstacles to integrate into our daily rhythms. Worth making a spiritual practice. Because when our lives bloom and flourish in the care of the Master Gardener, we will know and we will embody the abundant life Jesus promises His followers.

JOURNAL PROMPTS

Prompt 1

Set a five-minute timer and journal your response to this question: *Why do I want to journal?* Write without stopping for the full five minutes to keep your brain engaged, move past the conscious clutter, and tap into new ideas. Even if you need to write, "I don't know what to write next," or "My neighbor's loud noise is really bothering me," do it! Just keep going.

Prompt 2

First, make a list of 100 obstacles you face in making the journaling habit stick. This lengthy list may take twenty to thirty minutes to generate. But stick with it! Complete the whole list in one sitting, know that it's okay to repeat ideas on the list (this is part of the process and will help you actually get to 100), and move quickly (don't give yourself time to overthink).[5] As you look over your list, pick one obstacle to explore with *grace*, *compassion*, *curiosity*, and a *reframe*:

- *Grace:* Instead of self-judgment, what would grace say to me about this obstacle?
- *Compassion:* Write one sentence that validates the reality of the obstacle I'm facing.
- *Curiosity:* This obstacle feels like . . .
- *Reframe:* What's another way to see this obstacle or to see a way through this obstacle?

Prompt 3

Close your eyes. Breathe deeply. Allow yourself a few moments of quiet and stillness, where all you hear, all you feel, is your steady inhale and exhale. Ask God to open your imagination to Him.

I want you to imagine you are standing at the edge of the woods. It's a beautiful day, and you are dressed for a walk. The sun is warm on your skin, and the gentle breeze dances around your face.

As you stand at the edge of the woods, a path opens in front of you. The path is worn and smooth. You begin to walk down this path. Before long, you notice some of the path is rocky and uneven. You stoop down to look closely at the rocks, and you even scoop some into your hands. You rub your thumb over the surface of the rocks. You roll the pebbles around in your palm, considering how their weight feels in your hands.

You stand up and continue walking. You see a thorny patch of brambles, just ahead of you and off to the side of the path. A jumble of weeds and stalks, some with sharp thorns, is tangled together. The weeds and thorny vines have grown the tallest.

The path. The rocky soil. The thorny brambles. All are familiar to you. You've walked this path, sat in the rocky pebbled dirt, and even stood among the thorns before.

But today, you want to go a little further down the path. You want to push past this place and see what lies ahead. So, you continue to walk down the path. As you walk, you notice just a bit down the path a beautiful garden. The sun is filtering down through the leaves and branches. Beautiful trees and flowers wind their way through this garden.

In this garden, there is life. You are drawn by the light and beauty, the smells and the textures. To enter this garden, you must leave the rest of it behind. The beauty, the life, the goodness in this garden is like nothing you've ever seen before. The path here hasn't been easy. But now you've come all this way.

So, you enter the garden to experience its beauty. You drink in the colors, you rub your hand on the textures of the flowers and leaves, you take off your shoes to feel the soft, supple grass beneath your feet. You inhale the fragrance of this place.

Everywhere you look, there is life. There is goodness. You are overwhelmed by how prolific this garden has grown. You spend hours walking through this garden, touching every leaf, inhaling the scent of every petal, soaking in the layers upon layers of beauty.

Then, you notice in the middle of the garden a small wooden box, delicate and beautiful. Instinctively, you know this box is meant for you, left here by the One who tends this garden. As you make your way over to the box, your anticipation grows. You wonder what gift is in this box. You stop in front of the box and gently lift it in your hands. You breathe deeply and then open the box.

What gift do you find inside the box? Spend as much time as you need looking at, examining, exploring, and understanding the gift left by the Gardener for you. And when you're ready, put pen to page to write about your gift.

CHAPTER 9

Pursuing a Deeper Relationship with God: *The Vine and the Branches*

Spiritual formation helps us to see the face of God in the midst of a hardened world and in our own heart.

~Henri Nouwen

When we journal consistently as a spiritual practice, the fruit is having an identity rooted in Christ, the ability to trace the grace of God in our lives, and the reality of experiencing God's presence. Really, what we're talking about is deep, meaningful spiritual formation.

We can move from despair and disorientation to the full, abundant life. We can transform our emptiness into a full experience of the presence of God. We can fuel our spiritual appetites with the fullness of God. But it takes consistency and time.

Once, another special needs mom said that when disability grows up, it's no longer cute. People are less understanding of an angry, dysregulated teenager than they are of a chubby-fingered toddler who's signing "more" across the table to you at dinner.

These days, Reed's curly red mop meets my own five-foot-four frame eye to eye, and I could stare at his red hair all day. My favorite are the grannies who stop us in public to gawk over it. Granted, as a full-on teenager, Reed's a little less accommodating of their well-meaning compliments than when he was a toddler being pushed around in the cart at the grocery store.

But I know how soon people's compliments turn to quickly averted eyes when they witness how his anxiety lashes out at the world. The tension is palpable.

I find myself teetering over the edge of pity. My heart clenches and my mind swirls. I'm staring into a deep, familiar hole with few exits.

I wildly scan for something good, something light, that I can tether myself to. In my mind, I reach for my favorite one-liner when people remark on Reed's red hair: "I married my husband so I could have red-headed babies."

A small laugh bubbles up. Just enough to break the tension.

Then, the Spirit gently whispers, "He's the gift." The gift of a red-headed baby. The gift of my firstborn. The gift of showing me a new way to see the world. These words become a sheltering grace that lifts me back onto solid ground.

Sometimes we hold gifts that, frankly, don't feel like gifts. They seem like the wrong size, the wrong shape, the wrong everything. We can't help but think that if this is God's idea of a gift, we are pages apart.

And yet. God's practice is that of turning expectations upside down and inside out. What others feel only pity for, God whispers, "I'm here. I'm with you. And this is good."

God doesn't ask us to see the silver lining in the difficulties and the grief in our lives. He's asking us to see them through the lens of grace. Through tender mercy. As a road home to Him.

God doesn't ask us to see the silver lining in the difficulties and the grief in our lives. He's asking us to see them through the lens of grace.

Without the steady, consistent practice of journaling, these moments that threaten a downward spiral would be my undoing. How do I know this? Because Oxford Learning points out that "the process of writing by hand reinforces memory pathways and enhances comprehension and retention. This is a phenomenon well-documented in cognitive psychology."[1] Simply put, every time I take up my pen and ask God to help me rewrite my own inner narrative, He does just that, weaving His redemptive truth into my reality so that in those moments when I need it most, I have Him.

Every time I turn to Him, my heart takes on more of the shape of Him. Every time I hear the Holy Spirit's whisper, my soul more beautifully reflects Him. Every time I trace a line of His grace in my story, His love makes a home more deeply in the depths of who I am.

What Is Spiritual Formation?

We can understand the general idea of formation by looking at our lives. If you were born in the United States, you likely value your individual freedoms and the idea that you can pursue whatever goals in life you want. Did someone sit you down to teach this to you? Probably not, but you learned it by the conversations you overheard growing up, the politics your parents discussed at the dinner table, and the advertising you saw during commercial breaks in your favorite TV shows. So much of who we are and the lives we lead are influenced by where we were born, who raised us, and the ideas we were exposed to. This is why childhood is called the *formative* years.

Our spiritual values are formed in similar ways. By the time I was five years old, my dad had been ordained as a Lutheran minister, and I spent my formative years—every Sunday—attending church, reciting the liturgy in Sunday services, and going through confirmation as a teenager to affirm my commitment to God and the church. Church was an easy, natural thing for me to be a part of because I couldn't remember a time when this wasn't the case.

But I had a friend with a vastly different experience. She told me, "I wish I'd grown up in church like you. I wish I understood the Bible the way you do. But it's all so strange and different to me." Her parents didn't attend church, so she rarely went. They didn't have conversations about the Bible or the impact it could have on your life. Church—and by extension Christianity—were not easy or natural things for her. Her heart and mind had been formed by a different set of values.

And yet, spiritual formation is more than just a passive experience of what happens around us. Dallas Willard teaches us that "We have to recognize that spiritual formation in us is something that is also done to us by those around us, by ourselves, and by activities which we voluntarily undertake."[2] While we cannot simply by our own effort be made more Christlike, God invites us to be active participants in our spiritual formation. We can engage in life-giving, soul-nourishing practices like journaling to learn, as Dallas Willard suggests, "how to receive [agape love] into the deepest part of [our] being[s]."[3]

A Recursive Process

Spiritual formation is not a once-and-done accomplishment. Rather, it is a process of making "every effort to add to your faith goodness; and to goodness, knowledge; and to knowledge, self-control; and to self-control, perseverance; and to perseverance, godliness; and to godliness, mutual affection; and to mutual affection, love" (2 Peter 1:5–7). Spiritual formation is a recursive process, a continual movement toward being known, uncovering new layers, confessing and repenting, and being made new *again*. It's a process we'll do all of our God-given lives.

A recursive process is neither linear nor a checklist or a set of milestones. It is both a way forward and a way backward. It is coming around again and again to the same idea, seeing it is familiar, but also knowing that this time, *you* are different. So, even though the issue is the same, you can now see it differently from your new position, and because you're seeing it new again, your inner self is shaped and reformed.

Writing is also a recursive process. I explain it like this to my college writing students. If you hope to jot off your writing in one sitting and then send your piece on its merry way, you will be disappointed and your writing will be disappointing.

Why? Because writing needs to move and breathe to flourish. Writing is not a formula to follow; it is a process, a practice. Sometimes, you will sit down to brainstorm and find that you have a whole draft ready to put down on paper. Other times, with a draft written, you will assume you're ready to revise. But then, upon rereading your words, you notice that one of your ideas is not quite right, but you're not sure why. Back to brainstorming, you go. With each stop and start, with each loop, with each step forward and backward, the idea is being formed, taking shape. And truthfully, you are being shaped by this process too.

> We must be willing to step backward to see with clarity and to move forward with courage and hope.

For many of my students, embracing a recursive—rather than draft-and-done—practice of writing is frustrating. They simply want to follow the steps and be finished. If they're unwilling to engage with this recursive process, they might produce some writing. But it will not be fully formed. It will not be the truest, best expression of what they mean or want it to be or what it could be.

Similarly, we must engage with the process of spiritual formation. We must recursively step into the stream of grace to be shaped and formed, again and again, in the same and yet different ways each time. We must be willing to step backward to see with clarity and to move forward with courage and hope.

We must be willing to come back again to the place we started and see it all fresh again, while keeping faith that we are being transformed. We must be willing to slough off the old and expose the tender new things. We must be willing to sit with what feels like the same old worn-out line and let it be rewritten into a line of grace. Again and again.

If we're unwilling to engage with this recursive process, we might change a little. But we will not be fully formed. We will not be the truest, best expression of who we are or what we want to be or who we could be.

When we do engage fully to this process of spiritual formation, we'll find that measure by measure, loop by loop, we are being formed into the beautiful image and grace bearers of Christ we deeply desire to be. It's how we will come to embody the supernatural love of Christ *in the deepest parts of our being.*

Journaling for Spiritual Formation

We need a way to stay engaged in the recursive process of spiritual formation, and journaling offers us one path into this process. When we write our way to the heart of God on the pages of our journals, we can see clearly before us what He's doing—the work of God in black and white on the page. We can trace the lines of grace and redemption He's writing into our stories. Joining the recursive practice of journaling with the recursive process of spiritual formation creates a beautiful synergy in our spiritual lives.

How Consistent Do You Have to Be?

You might be asking how consistent you must be with journaling to reap its rewards. I get it. We all lead full, busy lives. Truly, any amount of journaling is beneficial. James Pennebaker's proven method of journaling for healing requires just four twenty-minute sessions to show improvement in mental health and well-being. But like any habit or practice, we find greater outcomes with greater consistency.

People who know me well—like my sister and my husband—can tell when I haven't been journaling regularly. I'm more angsty, anxious, nervous, and out of sorts. It's like missing a dose of medicine. I can function. But I'm better when, with regularity, I take pen to page. For me, in my current season, consistent journaling consists of three to four times per week intentionally sitting down with pen and page. On Saturdays, I gather with my online journaling community for thirty minutes to journal. About every other day of the week, I spend thirty minutes in my journal.

Maybe that sounds like a lot to you. So, start where you are. What about five minutes twice a week? Or one thirty-minute session once a week? I think about friends of ours who are weightlifters. When, as a non-lifter, I look at their lifting routine, I'm overwhelmed. No way could I start where they are, with either the amount of weight they lift or even with the duration or tenacity with which they lift. A couple of years ago, knowing I was a total beginner, they created a lifting program for me: three times a week, three to four exercises for strength building, which took around fifteen to twenty minutes, using relatively light weights. It was the perfect fit for where I was in that season and gave me the right building blocks to expand as I went.

What we do consistently forms us. Consistently lifting weights builds strength. Consistently brushing our teeth keeps the dentist bill low. Consistently expressing gratitude rewires our brains in positive ways.

Consistently journaling builds our strength, our resilience, our inner fortitude, and our ability to be present in our lives. Journaling consistently helps us see recurring patterns in our lives that we might otherwise miss. Taking pen to page allows us to experiment with different ways of journaling to find new insights and perspectives. Over time, consistent journaling forms us in spiritually significant ways.

Benefits of Consistently Journaling with Metaphor

- When we journal consistently, metaphors expand our imagination for what is possible, hopeful, and true.
- When we journal consistently, metaphors give us narratives to build meaning into our stories.
- When we journal consistently, metaphors create a map for navigating wildernesses.
- When we journal consistently, metaphors create a template for pressing into the heart of God.
- When we journal consistently, metaphors help us create a cohesive story from fragmented dreams and disappointments.
- When we journal consistently, metaphors construct a familiar concept to build a path through the unknown.
- When we journal consistently, we discover how metaphors meet us right where we are, with what we know, and refract light from just the right angle to illuminate the darkness.
- When we journal consistently, we can see how metaphors become the "well woven narrative [as] a way to journey through the brokenness, to traverse and even map our sorrow, even to find its borders, rather than merely assent to it," that Sarah Clarkson describes.[4]

- When we journal consistently, metaphors help us map our way back to God.
- When we journal consistently, metaphors bring our senses alive, as their textures and colors, smells and sounds, bring us back to spiritual vibrancy.
- When we journal consistently, metaphors become, says Craig Ott, the "communicative bridges [that] open the door of our imagination and convey rich layers of meaning, relationships, and emotions."[5]
- Journaling through Scripture's metaphors shapes us more and more into those who have experienced and are living out of the fullness of God's presence.

The Common Ground Between Metaphor and Spiritual Formation

Metaphors and spiritual formation are a natural duo. The symbols inherent in metaphors help us explore the realities of our spiritual formation. The vine and branch metaphor in John 15 is a beautiful picture of spiritual formation for us to consider. Jesus says, "I am the true vine, and my Father is the gardener" (John 15:1). Here, Jesus uses a gardening or agricultural metaphor—once again knowing it would be familiar and accessible to His listeners—to symbolize how a relationship with God is nourished. The spiritual reality is conveyed almost instantaneously with this image of a vine and gardener: We must be connected to our source of nourishment (Jesus) to grow spiritually, as God forms and shapes us.

Similarly, metaphors transform our understanding in the same way that spiritual formation transforms us. In John 15:2, Jesus continues, "Every branch that does bear fruit he prunes so that it will be even more fruitful." Any of us who have been through a painful season or difficult experience likely found ourselves asking why. *Why am I going through this? What is God doing?* We can recognize the truth that plants need to be cut back, which seems paradoxical. How can less of something produce more of anything? But any gardener worth their salt knows this is the only way for a plant to truly flourish. The same is true in our relationship with God. In being pruned, we are transformed.

Our experience of Jesus is how we come to know God and how we flourish in that relationship.

Just as metaphors must be connected to an experience we're familiar with, true spiritual formation occurs as we are connected to God through our familiarity with Jesus. In John 15:4, Jesus continues, "Remain in me, as I also remain in you. No branch can bear fruit by itself; it must remain in the vine. Neither can you bear fruit unless you remain in me." Through these metaphorical words, we are connected to the familiar experience of a branch requiring a vine, which is connected to roots and thus soil and nutrients, in order to make fruit. To know God, to thrive in relationship with Him, we must be connected to Jesus, who "is the radiance of God's glory and the exact representation of his being" (Heb. 1:3). Our experience of Jesus is how we come to know God and how we flourish in that relationship.

Metaphors are layered in meaning to challenge our understanding, just as spiritual formation penetrates through the layers of our being to challenge and change us. Jesus warns, "If you do not remain in me, you are like a branch that is thrown away and withers; such branches are picked up, thrown into the fire and burned" (John 15:6). It's tempting to look at a garden in full bloom and focus only on the beauty, what is easy on the eyes. But gardeners know it takes removing the dead wood to truly let a garden flourish. Farmers know that, sometimes, to cultivate healthy soil, you must burn the field. The same is true for us spiritually. Jesus penetrates straight through our desire for an easy spiritual life and reminds us that there's no such thing.

Metaphors are gifted to us in the words we speak and understand, just as spiritual formation is significantly impacted by the words and stories we consume and speak. Proverbs 12:18 attests to this spiritual reality: "The words of the reckless pierce like swords, but the tongue of the wise brings healing." And all of it is "so that my joy may be in you and that your joy may be complete" (John 15:11). In this way, His love can reach the deepest parts of our being.

JOURNAL PROMPTS

Prompt 1

As you consider your life, who and what has shaped you most? In what ways—good and bad—have they formed you into the person you are today? If this question feels too open-ended, you can focus on one factor or person that formed you. Or, you can limit your journaling session to just five minutes.

Prompt 2

Place the tip of your pen in the middle of a journal page. Begin to draw a circle, but before closing the loop, extend the circle into a spiral. Continue the looping spiral until your page is filled with the spiral circle. Writing your entry around the curve of the circle, ponder this prompt: Am I beginning again? How am I being formed in faith, goodness, knowledge, self-control, perseverance, godliness, mutual affection, and love? In what ways am I stepping back for clarity, while also moving forward with hope and courage? How is this recursive spiritual process shaping me?

Prompt 3

Close your eyes. Breathe deeply. Allow yourself a few moments of quiet and stillness, where all you hear, all you feel, is your steady inhale and exhale. Ask God to open your imagination to Him.

In my childhood home, my mom hung a framed cross-stitch design in our hallway. She had stitched the oak tree, with the words beneath it declaring, "The greatest oak was once a little nut that held its ground." While I don't know much about grape vines, I know a little bit about oak trees.

Looking up at a towering oak, it's hard to imagine its humble beginnings. And yet, that is God's design. The oak tree, at first hidden, unfurls its seed, sends out tender shoots, forms roots, pushes upward through the soil, and as it grows taller and taller, branches begin to grow and expand. Through each season, as long as that oak tree is connected to its roots and takes in nutrients of sun and soil, it continues to grow, to live, to thrive. Apart from that connection, the oak tree would wither and die. If that oak tree could tell its story, we'd probably be in awe of the storms and seasons it weathered, especially seeing its beauty now.

We're not so different from grape vines or oak trees, really. We need strong roots, good nutrients, and a deep and abiding connection to God. If we consider our own seasons, if we look closely and listen intently, we'll be able to tell the story of God with us each step of the way.

Begin to look over the course of your life. Imagine yourself as a small seed, unfurling in the soil, growing roots and pushing upward, extending out. Bring to mind the moments and experiences that have shaped you, both in hard and beautiful ways. As these come to mind, you may want to write them down in your journal, even if it's just as a list. If you can, grow your list to ten to twelve memories.

As you consider the path of your life, the course it has taken, the rough edges, the new growth, the gnarled knots, the beauty growing right out of you, can you trace the lines of grace that have been writing your story? Can you see how God has been with you all along the way? Can you sense your roots growing deeper into Him as you consider how He has gently and lovingly tended to you through the course of your life?

Give yourself time to simply be in His presence, seeing Him with you through it all. There's no rush. Only unhurried moments in the presence of our faithful Vinedresser. When you're ready, journal what you've just experienced.

CHAPTER 10

Life Is Short, Hard, and Beautiful:

How to Make Your Words Count

Hope is the thing with feathers that perches in the soul.

~Emily Dickinson

This feels embarrassing to admit, but Ben and I lived in eleven different houses over the span of just nine years. These moves were primarily voluntary, and sometimes? Just for a change of scenery. Novelty. Greater convenience or comfort.

I love perusing Zillow (perhaps I should have been a realtor) and easily feel the pull for a new project or a new space to make a home. "Oh, the Byxbes are moving again!" became a running joke of sorts among our friends through the years.

This year, though, will mark seven years of living in the same house, a milestone in our marriage. When we moved into this 1960s-era home, replete with its shag carpet and avocado-green tiled bathroom, I dubbed it Gardendale Roots and began telling friends that this was our forever house. I had finally reached a point where settling in became appealing. Maybe it's my ever-nearing approach to middle age or the fact that I have three kids and a dwindling supply of energy. But, changing houses like it's my job no longer holds the same appeal.

I feel the deep-down craving for establishing roots. Instead of moving on to the next new thing, I want to find contentment in what surrounds me. I want to settle into the routine, and yes, sometimes the monotony, of the same place, same people, same old same old, each and every day. As I grow older and settle into the long-haul rhythm of midlife, what I once viewed skeptically, I now want. We desire a place we can really call home, a place our children will point back to one day and say, "That was the house I grew up in."

We're inundated with marketing that wants to sell us on the next adventure, the next promotion, the next best thing. We're sold on the value of new, bright, and shiny over the known, mundane, and ordinary. But what if by settling in right where we are, we actually find the sacred and holy in all that is right here?[1]

This is the picture Moses paints of God in Psalm 90:1: "Lord, you have been our dwelling place throughout all generations." God is our home, our refuge. When we look back over the course of our lives, we can trace the line of grace and say, "God was my safe dwelling." God's story is bigger than just our own, though. He is a dwelling place not just for one person, not just for one moment of time. But for all of His people for all of time. Stronger than the mountains He created, He is God "from everlasting to everlasting" (Ps. 90:2). Our true home.

As beautiful as Psalm 90 is, Moses also lays out some hard truths. The kind of hard truths most of us would prefer to ignore, sweep under the rug, or not think about. Truths like, life is far shorter—just seventy or eighty years—than most of us like to really think about. And? Our brief lives are usually full of hardships, a clear marker of the disruption from the Fall.

God is a dwelling place for all of His people for all of time. Our true home.

Why does Moses open with this beautiful imagery of God being our dwelling place, our home, and our safe refuge, only to plunge us into the gritty, hard realities of life that most of us are far too acquainted with and would rather just not think about? I think Moses would be great at journaling with his wide-open honesty.

Verse 12 is our answer: "Teach us to number our days, that we may gain a heart of wisdom." If our lives are but a fleeting breath—if we will know strife, difficulty, and grief—then what on earth should we do? That bleak prognosis leads some to conclude that life is meaningless. But Moses has a different take. With a heart of wisdom, we can be satisfied by unfailing love, joy, and gladness, God's splendor, and the favor of the Lord on us and the work of our hands.

Have you spied the metaphor in verse 12? It's the first half of the verse: "Teach us to *number* our days." In our time-obsessed, number-crunching society, we might be tempted to take Moses literally. Count those days up! After all, he references that most people only get seventy or eighty years, so even he is counting in the literal sense of the word.

But Moses is after something more than just literally counting our days. Numbers are just facts, and facts do not birth wisdom. Michael Wilcock suggests, "The numbering of days is a lesson not in elementary arithmetic but in life-changing theology."[2] Like Jon Bloom, "I want to know what it means to grow wise as we grow older," and to do that, we have to understand that "God doesn't measure significance in terms of *time duration* but in terms of what he *values*."[3]

A Different Kind of Counting

My problem is that I spend too much time counting minutes instead of what God values. Time seems to rush me headlong into my days.

The alarm hasn't even gone off, but I hear my children fighting. *Sigh.* One peek in the mirror, and I know it's going to be a hopeless hair day. *Ugh.* "Mom! Where are my clean clothes?" I haven't even had coffee yet or rubbed the sleep from my eyes. "Babe, did you remember that I have that extra-long meeting tonight?"

I start mentally ticking through my to-do list, and then my I-really-ought-to-but-who-has-time-for-it list. *Time impatiently reminds me that I'll probably never get it all done.* Walking past my front door, I stand for a minute in the entryway, taking in the scattered socks, shoes, and other littered evidence of my kids. I eye the stack of dishes on the kitchen counter. I notice the two bills on the entryway table and the haphazard box that's been shoved under it for weeks, ready to be unpacked. I see my laptop screen blinking neon at me. My watch reminds me to "check my progress." *Time demands to know why I haven't done more.*

How will I use the time I have today? It feels as though if I make one wrong step, the whole day might implode. Will I have anything to show for the hours marked by the clock? Time and I circle each other in a wrestling match where I'm pinned, apt to lose. I can't tap out; I just have to keep moving. *Time is never my ally.*

Still, I ask: *Am I making the minutes of my life count?* Each ticking minute presses that question further into my heart, its sharp edges cutting deeply. If I had written Psalm 90:12, it'd go something like this: "You have taught her to number her days, *so that she could be anxious and twisted up in knots most of the time*."[4]

Anxiety is convinced that God will get the things in my life wrong. But wisdom know that abiding in Christ is what makes a life meaningful.

Anxiousness could well be called the antithesis of wisdom. Anxiety is convinced that God will get the things in my life wrong. Anxiety is convinced that doing more and being more productive will lend meaning to my life. But wisdom knows that in all things, God works for our good. Wisdom knows that abiding in Christ is what makes a life meaningful.

Wisdom flows from filtering our lived experiences through God's perspective and heart. H. C. Leupold defines wisdom this way: "Wisdom seems to consist in a full awareness of what is wrong with mankind and a full retreat to God as the only dwelling in this stormy existence where man can be safe."[5] Wisdom comes from tracing the lines of grace in our lives, drawing meaning out of our experiences, and trusting that He who began a good work in us will carry it to completion.

To number our days is to, yes, count them and see their brevity, but also to be wise about the realities of this life and the goodness of God. Moses instructs us to imagine that our days are well spent if from them we gain wisdom, not if we've conquered our to-do list.

The length or number of our days is not what satisfies us or creates joy or gladness. It is God's unfailing love, His deeds, His splendor, and His favor. We should count gifts, count on God's faithfulness, count on His unfailing love, count on His good deeds. We should count on seeing these lines of grace woven into our stories. A heart of wisdom comes from holding the counterweight of God's unfailing, everlasting love against our dust-to-dust lives. And one of the best ways to gain that wisdom? Journaling.

As we've explored, journaling through metaphor can become the shelter through which God rewrites the lines of our lives, allowing us to know His presence more fully. This practice invites us to know a reality where we are seen, known, and loved. This practice connects us to God, rewires our brains, rewrites our inner narratives, and cultivates peace and hope. This reality becomes the overflowing cup from which we love God and others.

I still have days when I must contend for my mental health. Where I must dig deep and grip God's hand like a scared, out-of-sorts toddler. Where I feel uncertain and unmoored. But I know where to go to reclaim my sanity. I know how to find His light in the darkness. And you better believe that's what I do. Because no feeling, no faltering, no flatlining is ever worth losing sight of Him and His life-giving presence in my day-to-day life.

There are still days where the overwhelming reality that I will always be a caretaker sits heavy on my heart. Where I'm overcome with sorrow for the ways in which this world will always present seemingly insurmountable challenges for Reed. Where I rail against the unfairness of it all. Where, as I've been known to tell Ben, I just don't want to do it anymore.

But I say with Jesus' beloved disciple Peter, "Lord, to whom shall we go? You have the words of eternal life" (John 6:68). I'm grounded in His resurrection, not in a diagnosis, a disaster, a disappointment, or a tomb. I relish knowing that on the other side of eternity, Reed will be healthy and whole, without the limitations of our present reality. What we can only see dimly now, we will see in all His radiant glory then. What here in this life has felt like heavy burdens will be revealed for the light and momentary afflictions they truly are. Or, to paraphrase Sam's question to Gandalf, all the sad things will become untrue.[6]

No feeling, no faltering, and no flatlining is ever worth losing sight of God and His life-giving presence in my day-to-day life.

Going Just One Step Further

Journaling, from a linguistic perspective, has its roots in the practice of conversing with God.[7] Expressing to God what we see reflected in our lives is a path that leads us to His presence. Journaling is a form of prayer, a conversation between you and God that reframes your perspectives, rewires your brain, and renews your mind. All by simply putting pen to page. This is one of the simplest and most accessible forms of soul care I know.

Reflecting on what I've journaled (so, yes, reflecting on my reflection) is one of the most transformative—and simple—practices I learned from Kathleen Adams at the Therapeutic Writing Institute. Doing so has cultivated more aha moments for me than I count!

Here's how it works: Once you've finished a journal entry, read back through it with curiosity and compassion. Just to see what you see. This is a practice of noticing. What do you notice about your thoughts, your feelings, your bodily sensations, your words on the page as you reread your entry? What questions crop up as you reread? What surprises you about what is (or, sometimes, is *not*) on the page? This is not a practice for judgment or condemnation, so ask your inner critic to take a back seat for this.

This is simply a practice to see what you see and make note of it. You might reread your entry with a highlighter in hand, marking interesting words, phrases, ideas, or connections. You might use a differently colored pen to make short notes in the margins about what you see or notice. You might simply write yourself an observation note at the end of the entry about what you noticed in the rereading. There's no right or wrong way to do this. You're simply invited to re-see with fresh eyes what you wrote in your journal. To trace the lines of grace that are holding your story together. You might even begin the practice by asking God to open your eyes as you reread, to see what He sees in your words.

A small note about *nothing.* Sometimes through the course of rereading your entry, you may see *nothing.* You may feel *nothing.* You may question *nothing.* At least nothing new. And that is okay. As a therapist told me once, sometimes *nothing* is the gift. Especially if you're prone to overanalyzing or overachieving. Your journal should be a place of rest and renewal, not another place where you feel pressured to perform or produce. Sometimes *nothing* is an invitation into rest, which is worth noting too.

A Prayer for When Life Is Hard

As we turn the last few pages of this book together, and as you prepare to journal the last few prompts, I want to share a prayer with you that I journaled as I finished writing this book. My hope is that it's an encouragement for you, a reminder of why journaling can be such holy work.

Oh Lord,

How much, how very much we long for a healed and whole reality. On the days the ache presses on us too hard, will You be with us? Help us to remain steadfast in the assurance of things hoped for, the assurance of things not yet seen or fully realized. And in this in-between, let us not forget that within us is Your river of living water. That because You reside in us, the kingdom is already here on earth. Though in the here and now we see in a mirror dimly, You are the true Light guiding us home.

In this meanwhile, we know there's good work to put our hands and hearts to. We know there are places to take the Light within us and mark the way for others. We know there's people and places that, through us, need to experience the love and gentleness of You, our Good Shepherd.

And so, with faith some days as tiny as a mustard seed, we keep turning to You and turning to the page and turning up for those who need us. Because in the turning to You and turning the page and turning up, we are being remade. Our stories are being rewritten, and the lines of grace we've been tracing are always leading us back to You.

No matter the hurricanes, earthquakes, or storms that may pass through our lives, we can know with unshakable certainty that You are with us.

JOURNAL PROMPTS

These last three journaling prompts are an invitation to revisit, reread, re-see—to trace the lines of grace now woven into the journaling you've done through this book. My prayer is that grace abundant will meet you in the reseeing and that as you trace those lines of grace, you will experience His presence anew.

Prompt 1

Review each of the prompts in this book. Which of your entries was your favorite and why?

Prompt 2

Take some time to read back through your journal entries you've written in response to the prompts for each book chapter. You may find it helpful to have a highlighter or other markers handy to annotate as you read. Ask for a heart of wisdom. Ask God to help you trace the lines of grace in your entries.

Reread with curiosity and compassion. Where do you see God's sheltering mercies? In what ways is God's unfailing love woven through your words? Where do you see joy and gladness? Do you notice any other patterns or themes in your entries? What thoughts or emotions rise within you as you reread your entries? What new insights, bridges, or connections do you notice in the rereading? What shifts, changes, or growth are evident in your entries?

Write down your observations, thoughts, notes to self, or prayers to God as a result of reading and reflecting on your entries.

Prompt 3

Close your eyes. Breathe deeply. Allow yourself a few moments of quiet and stillness, where all you hear, all you feel, is your steady inhale and exhale. Ask God to open your imagination to Him.

Bring to mind a calendar with today's date showing. Then slowly begin turning the pages of this calendar forward, to one year from today. As much as journaling is about reflecting on what has passed, it can also be about reflecting forward. To imagine, with God, what is possible.

Imagine that over the past twelve months, you have steadily put pen to page, tracing the lines of grace, and always at the end, finding that God is with you. *Emmanuel.*

You have developed a deeper intimacy with the Word Himself. Your life is flourishing because you abide with Him.

Imagine that you've fully embraced journaling as a daily or weekly spiritual practice. Through this practice, you have become profoundly in tune with God. You know His voice. You are experiencing fullness of joy because you have been with Him.

Write an entry celebrating the good things that have come from tracing the lines of God's grace through journaling as a spiritual practice.

P.S. Set a reminder on your phone for one year from today to come back and read this entry.[8]

Epilogue

When Your World Turns Purple

Looking over the activity-filled kid's menu, Reed hands me a crayon—the blue one (because he knows it's my favorite color). I draw a square of blue lines at the top of my page and begin to color it in, when he asks, "What's that?" I tell him I'm just doodling. With a mischievous smile spread wide, he scribbles over my blue lines with his red crayon, and beaming, says, "I messed up your picture!"

He is legitimately proud of himself. I pause for a beat. I stare at his addition to my art. I look over at his grinning face. "Oh, but you made it even more beautiful. You created purple." I smile back at him.

And I can't stop thinking about how true that is of our story together. Fourteen years ago, I was happily coloring in the lines of a normal, typical life. I had God in a perfect box. And I was just really fine and comfortable with both.

But God created this decidedly different boy who scribbles outside all of my comfortable, easy lines and shows me the stretching beauty of living outside the box and of trusting God when diagnoses bust up dreams and grief makes hearts all soggy.

Now, when I stop for just a minute and look at this wild, beautiful life I'm living, yes, I see the grief and ragged edges and turned down corners, but goodness I also see blazing, beautiful grace etched into every part.

I stop and I stare and realize, kinda slowly, purple might be my new favorite color after all.[1]

Appendix A

A Quick-Start Guide

to Journaling Through Metaphor

While the newness of journaling through metaphor might seem overwhelming to begin with, remember: We swim in an ocean of metaphor every single day. Like James Geary says, we speak "six metaphors a minute!"[1]

So, you're already familiar with the concept, but how do you know a metaphor when you see one? A metaphor often takes an everyday object or idea (such as a rock, light, vine, bread, or an animal) and transfers it to a person or a more abstract concept (such as God, Jesus, love, grace, or mercy). If you can insert the word "like" into the comparison, you've probably found a metaphor. For example, in Matthew 5:13, Jesus says, "You are the salt of the earth." Of course, we are not literally salt, and we can easily insert "like" into His sentence, and it makes sense: "You are [like] the salt of the earth."

Once you've identified the metaphor, answer the following questions in your journal:

1. What metaphor(s) have I found?
2. What words, ideas, or concepts surround this metaphor in the verses near it?
3. What truth, reality, or common experience does this metaphor build on?
4. How does this metaphor bridge to some aspect of who I am or an experience I've had?
5. What light does this metaphor shine on my thoughts, my own narrative about the difficulties I'm walking through?
6. How does this metaphor help connect fragmented parts of my story? How does this metaphor help me create meaning and insight in my story? What part of my story does this metaphor help heal?
7. What does this metaphor reveal about who God is and what He is like?
8. How does the metaphor deepen my understanding of and affection for God? How does it spark my holy imagination for what is possible, for what is good? How does this metaphor show or help me experience God's presence?
9. How does this metaphor help create a cohesive narrative that helps me find my way through my disappointment, loss, pain, grief, or other experiences and back to the heart of God?

If you're more of a visual learner, you could create a mind/heart map of what you associate with the central idea represented in the metaphor. See the image below for what this looks like (imagine filling in those blank bubbles with your own ideas and thoughts). In a mind/heart map, you place the central word/phrase in a circle in the center of your page. As you think of other words associated with that phrase, both those surrounding it in Scripture and your own connections, write those words down, circle them, and draw a line connecting them back to the central word/phrase. Write down as many connections/words as you can think of, and then study your mind/heart map. You could use the questions listed above to help you explore what shows up on your map.

Appendix B

Journaling Manifesto

Merriam-Webster defines a *manifesto* as a written declaration of a person's intentions.[1] Manifestos can be our written anchors, a way to reorient ourselves to the way forward. To remind ourselves of how valuable journaling is. To remind ourselves of the importance of journaling.

To journal is to . . .

- Trace the lines of grace and find that God has been here all along.
- Find a home for misplaced parts of us, build outposts for our tender places, and stitch patches over threadbare pieces.
- Hear His thoughts and soak them in.
- Tend to your soul as if it matters most.

- Nourish your life in this present moment.
- Press into this given moment and celebrate the beauty right here, right now.
- Rest your heart in Jesus.
- Slow down and pay attention to His heart.
- See that you are not yet who you ought to be, but in Him, you are becoming.
- Let grace rise higher than your insecurities.
- Know that life is not a problem to be solved or a crisis to manage through a white-knuckled death grip. Life is a gift to be lived in His good grip.
- Embrace how God is taking your messes, your dying hopes, and your washed-out wishes and making something good.
- Feel like you're cracking wide open, but know that it's Grace Himself cracking open deep wells of life within you.
- Believe revision isn't just a writing hack; it's a life-saving skill. Re-vision is re-seeing. And Grace is the Master Revisioner.
- Experience how death gives way to rebirth, and then rebirth gives way to life, and life gives way to hope.
- Know that in surrendering, you will rise again.
- Be assured that your grief is not lost on God.
- Tell your story because in telling, there is healing.
- Declare that God is authoring your story.

Acknowledgments

No author is an island, and this book is a testament to the grace and provision of God through the tapestry of people whose lives have been woven into mine.

To my parents, your love for reading and creative expression is stitched into every line of this book. Your unwavering love and support are gifts beyond measure. I love y'all.

Erin and JJ, no one laughs more at us than we do, and y'all kept me laughing through this whole long process. Lumi.

Mrs. Wardlaw, my third-grade teacher, thank you for being the first teacher to believe in my potential to read and write. Teachers will always be my first and favorite heroes.

When I first had the inkling I might have words to share with the world, I encountered two Ann(e)s—one whose book gave me permission to tell my story and the other whose book showed me a beautiful way to tell one's story.

My AV sister circle, y'all were right there with me when the idea for this book was born. From our year of creating together to the celebratory bouquet you sent me when I finished my book proposal to your consistent encouragement—there'll never be enough gratitude expressed.

Especially my dear, dear friend Deborah. Simply put, this book would not have been written without your weekly writing companionship. I'm so grateful for you, your wisdom, your encouragement, and your friendship. What a beautiful gift.

Evie, Sam, and Lauren—y'all were always just a text message or Marco Polo away. Our nearly lifelong friendship has been a buoy through so many seasons—and this season of writing a book was no different. When I doubted and when I celebrated, y'all were there. You have my infinite gratitude. Thank you for being some of the first to remind me that *Reed is nothing less and nothing more than a very special piece of me.*

The first two people (outside of my family) to believe in this book were Ann Kroeker and Don Pape. Writing a book is not easy. Being a first-time author is messy. You both put wind in my sails more times than I can adequately count. Thank you from the bottom of my heart (and inkwell). To the entire team at Moody—Trillia, Judy, Catherine, and Ashleigh—thank you for believing in, advocating for, and helping me make this book what it has become!

I'm also forever indebted to my Inky Collective and Saturday Pages journaling communities. To find other people who love journaling as much as I do? What a crazy, amazing gift!

I'm also indebted to the training I have received through the Therapeutic Writing Institute and Kay Adams, the founder of the Center for Journal Therapy, along with Kay's signature book *Journal to the Self*, without which this book could not have been written.

To the local expression of the church and the community groups and friends who have loved our family so beautifully, to name each of you would be a book all its own. But, our family loves those of you who have been Jesus with skin on to us.

Someone once asked me how, on top of being a wife, mother, professor, and journaling guide, I managed to write a book. *The answer is you, Ben.* Your gentle love and encouragement are the most beautiful reflection of our Heavenly Father and the reason I know deep down in my bones what it means to be truly seen, known, and loved. You'll always be my favorite yes.

Reed, Lucas, and Ansley, you have written more lines of grace into my story than I can even begin to count. I love you each so very, very much.

Notes

Introduction

Epigraph: William Wordsworth, *The Love Letters of William and Mary Wordsworth*, ed. Beth Darlington (Cornell University Press, 1981), 112.

1. Eugene Peterson, *Living the Resurrection: The Risen Christ in Everyday Life* (NAV Press, 2006), 84–85.

Chapter 1: The Potential of Metaphor: You Can't Pour New Wine into Old Wineskins

Epigraph: Anne Morrow Lindberg, "Introduction," in *Hour of Gold, Hour of Lead: Diaries and Letters of Anne Morrow Lindbergh, 1929–1932* (Harcourt Brace Jovanovich, 1973), 214.

1. This story first appeared in a blog post for PamelaHenkelman.com. See Allison Byxbe, "Allison's Story," https://www.pamelahenkelman.com/articles/refining-stories.
2. *Oxford English Dictionary*, s.v. "metaphor (*n.*)," December 2024, https://doi.org/10.1093/OED/3041519890.
3. Orson Scott Card, "Quest," in *Alvin Journeyman: The Tales of Alvin Maker IV* (Tom Doherty Associates, 1995), 42.
4. James Geary, *I Is an Other: The Secret Life of Metaphor and How It Shapes the Way We See the World* (Harper Perennial, 2012), 8.
5. Geary, *I Is an Other*, 5.
6. George Lakoff and Mark Johnson, *Metaphors We Live By* (The University of Chicago Press, 1980), 3.
7. *Merriam-Webster*, s.v. "metaphor (*n.*)," https://www.merriam-webster.com/dictionary/metaphor.
8. Aundi Kolber, *Try Softer: A Fresh Approach to Move Us Out of Anxiety, Stress, and Survival Mode—and into a Life of Connection and Joy* (Tyndale Momentum, 2020), 15.
9. Geary, *I Is an Other*, 181.
10. Eugene Peterson, *Tell It Slant: A Conversation on the Language of Jesus in His Stories and Prayers* (Wm. B. Eerdmans Publishing Co., 2008), 19.
11. Peterson, *Tell It Slant*, 24.

Chapter 2: The Presence of God Through Metaphor: The Unexpected, Gentle Whisper

Epigraph: J.D. Walt, "When God Whispers," *Seedbed*, September 9, 2022, https://seedbed.com/when-god-whispers/

1. Jonathan Peterson, "Why God Uses Metaphor to Describe Himself: Guest Post by Lauren Winner," Biblegateway, February 8, 2016, https://www.biblegateway.com/blog/2016/02/why-god-uses-metaphors-to-describe-himself-guest-post-by-lauren-winner/.
2. Craig Ott, "The Power of Biblical Metaphors for the Contextualized Communication of the Gospel," *Missiology: An International Review* 42, no. 4 (2014): 357–374, https://doi.org/10.1177/0091829613486732.
3. *Baker's Evangelical Dictionary of Bible Theology*, "Presence of God," by Bryan Beyer, accessed June 11, 2025, https://www.biblestudytools.com/dictionaries/bakers-evangelical-dictionary/presence-of-god.html.
4. "RTL Words: PANIM (פנים)," Right to Left Words, Iowa Bible & Archaeology, March 16, 2022, https://bam.sites.uiowa.edu/RTL/panim.
5. Tree Meinch, "We're Beginning to Understand the Power of Eye Contact," *Discover Magazine*, June 6, 2022, https://www.discovermagazine.com/mind/were-beginning-to-understand-the-power-of-eye-contact.
6. This is a paraphrase of 1 Kings 19:14.
7. Allison Byxbe, "His Presence, His Perspective," *The Glorious Table*, May 21, 2020, https://thegloriustable.wordpress.com/2020/05/21/his-presence-his-perspective-devotional/.
8. Sarah Clarkson, "A well-woven narrative can be a way to journey through the brokenness, to traverse and map our sorrow even to find its borders, rather than merely assent to it," Facebook, June 28, 2022, https://www.facebook.com/SarahEClarkson/posts/pfbid02SFPV6onUaBvYU5ofBswCp6k5wapZXAVuRCFq3aVRyWnSVfzRHhdNZr5o36BQSNPRl/.
9. Stacie Poston, "Purify Yourself," *The Advent Project 2022*, December 6, 2022, https://ccca.biola.edu/advent/2022/advent-2022-dec-6.

Chapter 3: The Power of Journaling: Our Mirrors Matter

Epigraph: Thomas Merton, New Seeds of Contemplation (New Directions Book, 2007), 60.

1. Alissa Quartz, "Bootstrapping Has Always Been a Myth. The New American Dream Proves It," *Time*, March 10, 2023, https://time.com/6261476/bootstrapping-myth-new-american-dream/.
2. Tim Keller, "American Christianity Is Due for a Revival," *Atlantic*, February 5, 2023, https://www.theatlantic.com/ideas/archive/2023/02/christianity-secularization-america-renewal-modernity/672948/.
3. Pete Briscoe, "Depending on a Completely Dependable God," November 19, 2024, https://www.petebriscoe.org/devotionals/depending-on-a-completely-dependable-god/.
4. The Genazzano Institute, "The Brain and Writing," LinkedIn, October 10, 2023, https://www.linkedin.com/pulse/brain-writing-the-genazzano-institute/.
5. Adam Young, "Why Engaging Your Story Heals Your Brain," accessed October 1, 2024, https://adamyoungcounseling.com/why-engaging-your-story-heals-your-brain/.

6. Ibid.
7. James Pennebaker, *Writing to Heal: A Guided Journal for Recovering from Trauma and Emotional Upheaval* (Center for Journal Therapy, Inc., 2013), 6–10.
8. Anne Morrow Lindbergh, *Hour of Gold, Hour of Lead: Diaries and Letters of Anne Morrow Lindbergh, 1929–1932* (Harcourt Brace Jovanovich, 1973), 214.

Chapter 4: The Potency of Journaling and Metaphor: Burying Seeds

Epigraph: William A. Ward, "Pertinent Proverbs by William A. Ward," *Fort Worth Star-Telegram*, (May 26, 1967), 4-D, Column 6.

1. Allison Byxbe, "Rising Again," *The Glorious Table,* April 9, 2020, https://thegloriousstable.wordpress.com/2020/04/09/rising-again-easter-devotional/.
2. Allison Byxbe, "The Unexpected Gift of Motherhood," *The Glorious Table*, November 2021, https://thegloriousstable.com/2021/11/unexpected-gift-of-motherhood/.
3. Allison Byxbe, "I gently take these seeds, push them into the ground. I bury what was because they only what dies can come to life." Facebook, January 28, 2023, https://www.facebook.com/photo/?fbid=10159546941958661&set=a.10150878816518661.
4. Allison Byxbe, "The Wild Beauty of Resurrection," *The Glorious Table*, May 14, 2019, https://thegloriousstable.wordpress.com/2019/05/14/wild-beauty-of-resurrection-devotional/.
5. Pat Schneider, *How the Light Gets In: Writing as a Spiritual Practice* (Oxford University Press, 2013), 57.
6. Christian Jarrett, "Life Is Different for People Who Think in Metaphors," The British Psychological Society, October 21, 2015, https://www.bps.org.uk/research-digest/life-different-people-who-think-metaphors.

Chapter 5: Light as Metaphor: Seeing the Goodness of God

Epigraph: Pat Schneider, *How the Light Gets In: Writing as a Spiritual Practice* (Oxford University Press, 2013), 75.

1. Denise Fornier, "Why We Should Stop Running from Pain," *Psychology Today*, August 2, 2020, https://www.psychologytoday.com/us/blog/mindfully-present-fully-alive/202008/why-we-should-stop-running-pain.
2. Allison Byxbe, "The Unexpected Gift of Motherhood," *The Glorious Table*, November 2011, https://thegloriousstable.com/2021/11/unexpected-gift-of-motherhood/.
3. Dane Ortlund, *Gentle and Lowly: The Heart of Christ for Sinners and Sufferers* (Crossway, 2020), 48.
4. Allison Byxbe, "The Unseen Christ," *The Glorious Table*, December 2021, https://thegloriousstable.com/2021/12/the-unseen-christ/.

5. Phyllis Klein, "The Healing Power of Therapeutic Writing and Poetry," Women's Therapy Services, September 21, 2013, https://womenstherapyservices.com/healing-power-therapeutic-writing-poetry/.
6. Quina Aragon, "The Psalms Through the Eyes of a Modern-Day Poe," August 2020, https://annvoskamp.com/2020/08/the-psalms-through-the-eyes-of-a-modern-day-poet/.
7. Abbey Houde, "Shifting your thoughts and perspective is a great start, but to really make a difference in your brain, you need to act on it!" Instagram, January 18, 2025, https://www.instagram.com/p/DE7e2kvRwpv/?locale=ko&hl=en.
8. Allison Byxbe, "My niece led me to the turbulent waters of immense, life-altering loss. She became the first whispers that even in our darkest pain," Instagram, July 20, 2020, https://www.instagram.com/p/Cu65qkDuk08/?utm_source=ig_web_copy_link&igsh=MzRlODBiNWFlZA==.
9. *Merriam-Webster*, s.v. "light (*n.*)," https://www.merriam-webster.com/dictionary/light.

Chapter 6: The Path to Healing: Leaving Shame at the Well

Epigraph: Ann Voskamp, ". . . maybe on the days we want out of our lives — it isn't so much that we want to die from shame, but 'hide' from shame," Facebook, March 6, 2017, https://www.facebook.com/photo.php?fbid=1497686953576807&id=324577877554393&set=a.369461463066034.

1. Brené Brown, "Shame vs. Guilt," January 15, 2013, https://brenebrown.com/articles/2013/01/15/shame-v-guilt/.
2. Robb Moll, "How Neuroscience—and the Bible—Explain Shame: Interview by Rob Moll," *Christianity Today*, July/August 2016, https://www.christianitytoday.com/2016/06/how-neuroscience-and-bible-explain-shame/.
3. Ibid.
4. Deborah Ross and Kathleen Adams, *Your Brain on Ink: A Workbook on Neuroplasticity and the Journal Ladder* (Bloomsbury Publishing, 2016), 19.
5. Tim McKee, "The Geography of Sorrow: Francis Weller on Navigating Our Losses," *The Sun Interview*, October 2015, https://www.thesunmagazine.org/articles/27277-the-geography-of-sorrow.
6. Moll, "How Neuroscience—and the Bible—Explain Shame."
7. Ibid.
8. Ibid.
9. Ibid.
10. Ross and Adams, *Your Brain on Ink*, 17.
11. Carly Mallenbaum, "Blue Mind: Why We Find the Water Peaceful," Axios, July 2, 2024, https://www.axios.com/2024/07/03/blue-mind-water-data-peaceful.

Chapter 7: The Practice of Journaling: Come to the Table

Epigraph: Eugene Peterson, *Christ Plays in Ten Thousand Places* (Wm. B. Eerdmans Publishing Co., 2005), 206, 212.

1. James Clear, "How to Start New Habits That Actually Stick," accessed May 15, 2025, https://jamesclear.com/three-steps-habit-change.
2. Ceri Perkins, "The Neuroscience of Beauty: What Your Brain Finds Beautiful—and How This Shapes Your Thoughts," *BBC Science Focus*, April 16, 2023, https://www.sciencefocus.com/science/the-neuroscience-of-beauty.
3. Michael Hyatt, "How to Make a New Habit Stick," *Full Focus*, accessed May 15, 2025, https://fullfocus.co/make-a-new-habit-stick/.
4. Kathleen Adams, *Journal to the Self: Twenty-Two Paths to Personal Growth—Open the Door to Self-Understanding by Writing, Reading, and Creating a Journal of Your Life* (Grand Central Publishing, 1990), 76.
5. PsychCentral, "ADHD Body Doubling," May 11, 2022, https://psychcentral.com/adhd/adhd-body-doubling.
6. Ann Voskamp, "About What's Better than To-Do Lists, & How to Have Spiritual Habits That Change Your Life," Ann Voskamp, May 2022, https://annvoskamp.com/2022/05/about-whats-better-than-to-do-lists-how-to-have-spiritual-habits-that-change-your-life/#:~:text=wear%20our%20days.-,If%20you%20consistently%20keep%20the%20same%20rhythms%20every%20day%20you,through%20the%20waves%20of%20life.
7. Ru Kotryna, "sometimes your body is asking for wood, for water, for the kindness of round things—this is a nervous system remembering what safe feels like," April 21, 2025, https://www.instagram.com/p/DItYnbAOX_g/?igsh=MTd5N20xbmk5ZW1uZw%3D%3D&img_index=4
8. Barry Jones, "The Dinner Table as a Place of Connection, Brokenness, and Blessing," *DTS Magazine*, October 26, 2015, https://voice.dts.edu/article/a-place-at-the-table-jones-barry/.
9. Allison Byxbe, "He Is the Bread of Life," *The Glorious Table*, March 10, 2022, Table, https://thegloriousTable.wordpress.com/2022/03/10/he-is-the-bread-of-life/.
10. Jones, "The Dinner Table as a Place of Connection, Brokenness, and Blessing."
11. Allison Byxbe, "Come to the Table," *The Sacred Ezine*, November 2022, 47.

Chapter 8: Pushing Through Obstacles: Keeping Pen to Page

Epigraph: Gretchen Rubin, "Little Happier: Habits Are the Invisible Architecture of Everyday Life," *Happier with Gretchen Rubin* podcast, July 20, 2020, https://gretchenrubin.com/podcast/little-happier-habits-are-the-invisible-architecture-of-life/.

1. Allison Byxbe, "How do you live when the grief is a long, living grief? When you wake up to the kind of new that rewrites, redefines, repurposes your life. A grief you don't outgrow," June 21, 2023, https://www.instagram.com/p/Ctxs4ccsgyE/?utm_source=ig_web_copy_link&igsh=MzRlODBiNWFlZA==

2. The Chara Project, "The Parable of the Sower," accessed May 15, 2025, https://www.thecharaproject.com/blog/parable-of-the-sower.
3. Ibid.
4. Dallas Willard, "Spiritual Formation: What It Is, and How It Is Done," Dallas Willard Ministries, accessed June 1, 2025, https://dwillard.org/resources/articles/spiritual-formation-what-it-is-and-how-it-is-done.
5. The instructions for this prompt are based on the List of 100 concept described by Kathleen Adams in chapter 12 "Lists" of her book *Journal to the Self* and from the training I have received as part of the Certified Journal Facilitator credential at the Therapeutic Writing Institute.

Chapter 9: Pursuing a Deeper Relationship with God: The Vine and the Branches

Epigraph: Henri Nouwen, *Spiritual Formation: Following the Movements of the Spirit* (HarperOne, 2010), xxix.

1. Oxford Learning, "How Writing by Hand Boosts Memory and Learning," March 29, 2024, https://oxfordlearning.com/how-writing-by-hand-boosts-memory-and-learning/.
2. Dallas Willard, "Spiritual Formation: What It Is, and How It Is Done," Dallas Willard Ministries, accessed May 15, 2025, https://dwillard.org/resources/articles/spiritual-formation-what-it-is-and-how-it-is-done.
3. Ibid.
4. Sarah Clarkson, "A well-woven narrative can be a way to journey through the brokenness, to traverse and map our sorrow even to find its borders, rather than merely assent to it," Facebook, June 28, 2022, https://www.facebook.com/SarahEClarkson/posts/pfbid02SFPV6onUaBvYU5ofBswCp6k5wapZXAVuRCFq3aVRyWnSVfzRHhdNZr5o36BQSNPRl/.
5. Craig Ott, "The Power of Biblical Metaphors for the Contextualized Communication of the Gospel," *Missiology: An International Review* 42, no. 4 (2014): 357–74, https://doi.org/10.1177/0091829613486732.

Chapter 10: Life Is Short, Hard, and Beautiful: How to Make Your Words Count

Epigraph: Emily Dickinson, "Hope Is the Thing with Feathers," in *The Complete Poems of Emily Dickinson*, accessed August 7, 2025, https://www.poetryfoundation.org/poems/42889/hope-is-the-thing-with-feathers-314.

1. Allison Byxbe, "Settling In," *The Glorious Table*, September 2, 2020, https://thegloriоustable.wordpress.com/2020/09/02/devotional-settling-in/.
2. Michael Wilcock, "Book IV (Psalms 90–106), in *The Message of Psalms 73–150, The Bible Speaks* (InterVarsity Press, 2001), 77.
3. Jon Bloom, "Life Is Too Brief to Waste: Learning to Number Our Days," Desiring God, September 8, 2024, https://www.desiringgod.org/articles/life-is-too-brief-to-waste.
4. Allison Byxbe, "God's Gift of Time," *The Glorious Table*, May 16, 2022, https://theglorioustable.wordpress.com/2022/05/16/gods-gift-of-time/.

5. H. C. Leupold, *Exposition of The Psalms* (Baker Book House, May 1981), 647.
6. J. R. R. Tolkien, *The Return of the King: Being the Third Part of The Lord of the Rings* (Mariner Books, 1994), 930.
7. Oxford Languages, s.v. “journal,” accessed June 11, 2025, https://rb.gy/exfhtc.
8. This prompt is based on the concept of a perspectives journal entry found in chapter 18 “Perspectives” in Kathleen Adams’ book *Journal to the Self.*

Epilogue

1. Allison Byxbe, “Looking over the activity-filled kid’s menu, Reed hands me a crayon—the blue one (because he knows it’s my favorite color). I scribble some blue lines at the top of a page,” Facebook, January 13, 2024. https://www.facebook.com/share/p/1DRePWSAYm/

Appendix A: A Quick-Start Guide to Journaling Through Metaphor

1. James Geary, *I Is an Other: The Secret Life of Metaphor and How It Shapes the Way We See the World* (Harper Perennial, 2012), 5.

Appendix B: Journaling Manifesto

1. *Merriam-Webster*, s.v. “manifesto (*n.*),” https://www.merriam-webster.com/dictionary/manifesto.